OXFORD REVISION GUIDES

GCSE

ENGLISH
for London Examinations

Pam Taylor

Chief Examiner, GCSE English

OXFORD
UNIVERSITY PRESS

OXFORD

UNIVERSITY PRESS

Great Clarendon Street, Oxford OX2 6DP

Oxford University Press is a department of the University of Oxford.

It furthers the University's objective of excellence in research, scholarship,
and education by publishing worldwide in

Oxford New York

Athens Auckland Bangkok Bogota Buenos Aires Calcutta
Cape Town Chennai Dar es Salaam Delhi Florence Hong Kong Istanbul
Karachi Kuala Lumpur Madrid Melbourne Mexico City Mumbai
Nairobi Paris São Paulo Singapore Taipei Tokyo Toronto Warsaw

with associated companies in Berlin Ibadan

Oxford is a registered trade mark of Oxford University Press
in the UK and in certain other countries

© Oxford University Press 1999

First published 1999

ISBN 0 19 831 4590 (student's edition)
ISBN 0 19 831 4604 (bookshop edition)

Packaged by Aldridge Press
Designed by Geoffrey Wadsley
Edited by Janey Fisher and Jenny Vaughan
Typeset in Garamond
Printed in Great Britain

contents

CONTENTS

general introduction

A way forward

How will this book support you in your aim of doing well in English? We hope you will find it:

- useful in preparing you for your Edexcel GCSE English examinations;
- a helpful aid to your reading of the selected texts from *Tracks*, explaining some of the difficult points.

Above all, it should be:

- an aid to develop your own thinking and responses;
- a stimulus for discussion;
- a clear system for your revision.

The first half of the book goes through each of the requirements for the two examination papers, with explanations, suggestions and questions. The second half gives you sample questions, answers and commentaries.

> ***Remember***, *the sooner you organise your thoughts and ideas, the easier you will find the preparation for all parts of the examination!*
>
> *This book aims to give you* **CONFIDENCE**.
>
> *You know you can succeed.*

ideas and approaches

Using your book
Here are a few ideas on how you might use this book.

Know your texts
It is very important to make sure that you have a really good grasp of the selected poems and non-fiction passages from *Tracks*. Every year, examiners read GCSE scripts where the candidates write in a way which shows that they do not understand, or have not prepared carefully, the texts which are set. Use the sections from this book to strengthen your knowledge of the texts.

Know your technical terms
As do all other subjects, English has a number of technical terms which you may need to use. It is important that you can use the correct term and that you can spell it. (Please refer to the useful glossaries on pages 39, 56 and 81.)

Know the types of writing required
These are:
- inform, explain, describe (see page 50);
- analyse, review, comment (see page 71);
- argue, persuade, instruct (see page 72).

Explore how to improve the structure and organisation of your answers. If you look closely at the model answers on pages 34–8, 52–5 and 75–80 and the examples of answers at different grades (pages 82–94) this will help you to write detailed, successful responses.

Presenting your work effectively
How you set out your own writing is important for various reasons. Get into the habit of producing writing that is:
- neat, regular and clear;
- spelt accurately;
- correctly punctuated;
- set out in clear paragraphs;
- laid out and presented well.

Apart from being good in themselves, such qualities in your writing will bring many benefits and advantages, both in the examination and afterwards.
- Examiners will form a positive impression of your work.
- They will not be slowed down or confused, as they will if the writing is hard to read and not written in proper sentences.
- How you write as well as what you write will be taken into account when your work is marked.
- Good writing is useful for applications for jobs or college courses.
- Many jobs need people who can write clearly, accurately and precisely.

Knowing your own strengths and weaknesses

It is an excellent idea to keep a checklist of your most common errors in spelling, punctuation and grammar.

○ When you receive a piece of work back from your teacher, read it through and make sure you understand any comments or corrections.
○ Keep a sheet of file paper at the front or back of your work file and write down on it the correct spelling of words you have misspelt.
○ Refer to this before handing in your work, to make sure you have not made the same mistakes.
○ Take some time to learn the correct spelling of all words on this list and check any points on punctuation and grammar you have noted.

Approach during your English course

Pay attention!

○ Listen to what teachers say.
○ Concentrate during class or group discussion.
○ Make certain you know what you have to do in class.
○ Be sure you understand what the homework is.
○ Check what your coursework assignments are.

Take part!

○ Ask questions in class.
○ Answer questions in class.
○ Contribute to discussion.
○ Be fully involved in group work.

(Your grade could depend on it!)

Make notes!

○ Keep clear records.
○ Write down key points from:
  teachers
  books you read
  class work
  articles or worksheets.
○ Annotate *Tracks* carefully (with your own interpretations).
○ Add points missed onto the end of your homework or practice questions when they are returned to you.

Keep up!

○ Hand work in on time.
○ Keep files or exercise books up to date.
○ Make sure homework does not get behind.
○ Do not leave work unfinished. (It is always difficult to remember what has been missed unless you amend it at the time.)
○ Check off completed work in your records.

Seek help!
○ Ask teachers to explain if you are unsure.
○ Discuss with friends.
○ Look things up by using:
   dictionaries
   encyclopædias
   the Internet.

Be organised!
○ Have clear systems.
○ Present work clearly.
○ Set yourself targets.
○ Stick to deadlines.
○ Keep your files neat and your notes together.
○ Organise yourself as you go through the course, as this is much better than trying to catch up at the last moment.

Approach to revision

Revising for examinations is a subject written about in many books, and these offer different suggestions and advice. What is certain is that not everything works for everyone. Each person has particular ways of revising and habits of working. Look at all the advice and try out the different suggestions. Decide clearly what are the **knowledge**, **skills** and **techniques** which you need to **acquire**, **develop**, **consolidate** or **revisit**.

What has to be done?
There are several steps.
○ Define the task.
○ Split it into its different parts or stages.
○ Identify your strengths and weaknesses.

Planning a schedule
○ Draw up a table to show the days and weeks before the examination.
○ Decide how much time to give to the subject in each week or day.
○ Work out a timetable with reasonable blocks of time.
○ Think about the need for variety and breaks.
○ Make sure your schedule is building towards a 'peak' at the right time.

How to improve
○ Test yourself.
○ Test a friend.
○ Practise examination questions.
○ Write to time limits, based on those in the actual examination.
○ Check your understanding of all texts, looking at words, meaning, plot and character.
○ Revise technical terms, using a **glossary**.
○ Be sure you can apply these properly, spell them properly, give examples, and explain how and why they are used.

Aids to learning

Write short, clear notes. Use such aids as:

- postcards
- diagrams
- flowcharts
- mnemonics (aids to memory, such as rhymes)
- computer programs
- audio tapes.

Other people

Do not try to go it alone. Ask others to check your progress, including:

- teachers
- parents, aunts or uncles
- elder or younger brothers/sisters
- classmates/friends.

Approach to exams

The whole of this book is designed to help you to approach the GCSE examinations in English with as much confidence as possible. Everyone knows that grades in the GCSE are regarded as being of great importance by many people. Particular courses of study, and very many forms of employment, require particular grades. This is especially true of English and Mathematics, which are basic requirements for all sorts of future occupations.

The importance of GCSE grades can create a sense of pressure. If managed properly, this can help your approach considerably, but if you're not careful it may also lead to too much worry and damage your performance.

Good preparation

Good preparation is one of the main elements affecting how people perform in examinations. This includes both attitude of mind and physical preparation.

1 Attitude of mind:
- Be positive.
- Be ready.
- Be calm.

2 Physical preparation:
- Be fit.
- Be alert.
- Be awake.

There are also specific things you need to do once in the examination room.

Come well-equipped

- Bring pens, pencils, rubbers, rulers and your copy of *Tracks*.
- Arrive in plenty of time.

Prepare and plan
- ○ Take 5 to 10 minutes to check instructions and read the paper carefully.
- ○ Decide how much time you need to allocate to each question. (You should aim to give about the same amount to each question, leaving five to ten minutes for checking through at the end.) Each English paper lasts two hours. An example of how to plan your time is shown below.

Reading the question paper	Question 1	Question 2	Question 3	Final Checking
5 mins	Planning – 5 mins Writing – 30 mins	Planning – 5 mins Writing – 30 mins	Planning – 5 mins Writing – 30 mins	10 mins
120 minutes (2 hours)				

- ○ Write a brief plan for each answer (approximately 5 minutes).
- ○ Look at any **key words** in the question, such as **compare**, **discuss** and **analyse**.
- ○ Do not just copy out prepared notes, since they will not allow you to do the most important thing of all: **answer the question**.

Check your work
- ○ Check that you are keeping to your planned timings.
- ○ Keep thinking throughout about:
  - Relevance
  - Presentation
  - Accuracy
  - Varied vocabulary.

With your time at the end:
- ○ Make sure you have answered all questions fully and appropriately.
- ○ Correct any errors in **spelling** or **punctuation** (check, especially, that all sentences have full stops).
- ○ Be certain everything can be read clearly.

Planning an answer

Answer the question!

Do not just write down everything you know! (This is the most common mistake made by examination candidates.)

Planning consists of the following elements:
- ○ reading the question carefully and recognising what are the key words in it;
- ○ deciding the main points you wish to make (what the question is looking for and how you intend to tackle it);
- ○ selecting what you wish to include in the answer;
- ○ giving your answer a structure: **introduction**, **main section(s)** and **conclusion**;
- ○ choosing examples or quotations.

Thinking about the question

Identifying the **key words** in the question can help to show:

- what the question is looking for; and
- how you intend to tackle it.

Key words show what the examiner is expecting in setting this task. (There are often bullet points to help you.) For example:

- **Describe** asks you to show fully what you know about the content or character.
- **Explain** asks you to make clear to the examiner your understanding of the writing.
- **Discuss** invites you to weigh up both sides of an argument and come to your *own* conclusion.
- **Analyse** expects you to look closely and in detail at the writing and its effects.
- **Compare and contrast** asks for an examination of similarities and differences.
- **Give an appreciation of** seeks your personal response to the qualities of the writing.

Some of these words are covered in the sections from page 71 to page 73.

Key points

Write down quickly, in note form, your immediate thoughts about the subject. (You may find a diagram useful for this purpose.) Do not write full sentences here, or you will waste too much time.

The content of the answer

Try to include the following (the 'five vowels' mnemonic **A, E, I, O, U** may help you):

- **analysis**
- **ideas**
- **understanding.**
- **evidence**
- **opinions**

The examiner does want to know what you think: your own, personal **ideas** and **opinions**. But a series of unsupported statements starting with the words 'I think' is **not** enough, since the examiner also needs to know on what these ideas are based: the **analysis** of language and content, the **understanding** of the subject-matter, and the **evidence** on which your views are based.

Deciding the structure: introduction, main section(s) and conclusion

Introduction: A clear, brief introductory paragraph can make a very good initial impression, showing the examiner that you are thinking about the actual question.

Main Section(s): Decide how many paragraphs or sections you wish your answer to contain.

Conclusion: This may be quite a brief paragraph. It should sum up clearly and logically the argument that has gone before. Above all, it should show the examiner that you have **answered the question!**

Using quotations

When writing about English passages, whether books, poems, articles or extracts, one of the most important things is to use quotations. This is a skill which has to be practised. Over-use of quotations is as bad a mistake as not using any. You should use quotations especially for the following reasons:

- to illustrate or give an example (e.g. a simile or an instance of alliteration);
- to explain why you believe something (to support an opinion or argument or to prove a point);

Quotations should be short (one word to a line or two at the most), relevant and effective. Introduce quotations fluently into your sentence structure. Avoid saying 'He says'.

poetry

Comparing and contrasting poems

On page 11, there was a reference to the fact that many questions ask you to 'compare and contrast' two poems. This section gives an example of two short poems, offered for comparison. These have been chosen so that you can think about how to set about such a comparison.

1 Read the two poems through at least twice. It is a very good idea to read them aloud once (or more). Most poems were written to be heard, and listening to their sound is an important part of understanding their meaning and effect. Check that you have grasped the basic ideas, and look up any words which you do not know in a dictionary.

When two poems are selected for this kind of comparison, there are usually some clear similarities – for example, of subject-matter – and also differences (such as the attitude of the poet towards this subject). This is true of the two poems on the opposite page.

It will help you to know that the two poems both come from the First World War (1914–1918). Rupert Brooke wrote 'The Soldier' right at the start of the war, before the trench warfare had commenced. Wilfred Owen wrote his 'Anthem for Doomed Youth' much later in the war (1917), after experiencing some of the worst of the battles, including the Somme. Think about the importance of this difference as you read the poems and respond to them. Underlining key words or phrases in different colours is one way to see which points you can link together, e.g. red for imagery, blue for attitudes to war.

2 Start with the obvious similarities:
   ○ Both are about war.
   ○ Both have 14 lines, one stanza of 8 and one of 6 (they are both sonnets).
   ○ Then look for other, perhaps less obvious subjects common to both, such as soldiers, death and burial.

3 Now think about the differences:
   ○ Brooke's is about himself, Owen's is about other people.
   ○ They show different attitudes to war and different attitudes to death.
   ○ Other differences:
        use of language
        rhyme and rhythm
        tone of voice.

4 In conclusion, think about your personal response:
   ○ Which poem do you prefer, and why?
   ○ Which makes the stronger impact, and how?

The Soldier

If I should die, think only this of me:
    That there's some corner of a foreign field
That is for ever England. There shall be
    In that rich earth a richer dust concealed;
A dust whom England bore, shaped, made aware,
    Gave, once, her flowers to love, her ways to roam,
A body of England's, breathing English air,
    Washed by the rivers, blest by suns of home.

And think, this heart, all evil shed away,
    A pulse in the eternal mind, no less
        Gives somewhere back the thoughts by England given;
Her sights and sounds; dreams happy as her day;
    And laughter, learnt of friends; and gentleness,
        In hearts at peace, under an English heaven.

Anthem for Doomed Youth

What passing-bells for these who die as cattle?
    Only the monstrous anger of the guns.
    Only the stuttering rifles' rapid rattle
Can patter out their hasty orisons.
No mockeries now for them; no prayers nor bells,
Nor any voice of mourning save the choirs, –
The shrill, demented choirs of wailing shells;
And bugles calling for them from sad shires.

What candles may be held to speed them all?
    Not in the hands of boys, but in their eyes
Shall shine the holy glimmers of goodbyes.
    The pallor of girls' brows shall be their pall;
Their flowers the tenderness of patient minds,
And each slow dusk a drawing-down of blinds.

Thomas Hardy (1840 – 1928)

Thomas Hardy was born at Higher Bockhampton, near Dorchester, Dorset. He is studied today for his novels (e.g. 'Tess of the D'Urbervilles', 'Jude the Obscure', 'Far from the Madding Crowd', 'The Mayor of Casterbridge') and for his poetry. Hardy published 'The Going of the Battery', about soldiers setting off on the long journey to fight in the Boer War, in a magazine, *The Graphic*. The following note was added: 'November 2, 1899. Late at night, in rain and in darkness, the 73rd Battery, Royal Field Artillery, left Dorchester Barracks for the War in South Africa, marching on foot to the railway station, where their guns were already entrained.'

The Going of the Battery

The Going of the Battery
Wives' Lament
(2nd November, 1899)

O it was sad enough, weak enough, mad enough –
Light in their loving as soldiers can be –
First to risk choosing them, leave alone losing them
Now, in far battle, beyond the South Sea!...

– Rain came down drenchingly; but we unblenchingly
Trudged on beside them through mirk and through mire,
They stepping steadily – only too readily! –
Scarce as if stepping brought parting-time nigher.

Great guns were gleaming there, living things seeming there,
Cloaked in their tar-cloths, upmouthed to the night;
Wheels wet and yellow from axle to felloe,
Throats blank of sound, but prophetic to sight.

Gas glimmers drearily, blearily, eerily
Lit our pale faces outstretched for one kiss,
While we stood prest to them, with a last quest to them
Not to court perils that honour could miss.

Sharp were those sighs of ours, blinded these eyes of ours,
When at last moved away under the arch
All we loved. Aid for them each woman prayed for them,
Treading back slowly the track of their march.

Some one said: 'Nevermore will they come: evermore
Are they now lost to us.' O it was wrong!
Though may be hard their ways, some Hand will guard their ways,
Bear them through safely, in brief time or long.

– Yet, voices haunting us, daunting us, taunting us,
Hint in the night-time when life beats are low
Other and graver things... Hold we to braver things,
Wait we, in trust, what Time's fulness shall show.

The Boer War
The Boer War was fought between the British and the Dutch settlers (Boers) in South Africa, between 1899 and 1902. The journey the soldiers had to travel to reach South Africa would, in those days, have taken several weeks.

Some features of the poem to study

Rhyme, rhythm and sound

The use of **rhyme** is one of the most striking features of the poem's construction:

- Study the rhyme scheme for each stanza (look at the end of every line).
- Look also for the use of **internal rhyme** on the **first** and **third** line of each stanza.
- Think especially about the first lines of the stanzas and notice the particular effect of the first line of the **first**, **middle** and **last** stanza. What does the **triple rhyme** here add to the effect?

The **rhythm** (metre) of the poem is regular throughout. Hardy uses a series of **feet** (a foot is a metrical unit) consisting of one heavy (stressed) and two light (unstressed) syllables. This foot is known as a **dactyl** and can be thought of simply as *tum*-te-te.

- How does this regular dactylic rhythm relate to the movement of the poem? (Think of such words as 'They stepping steadily' and 'trudged on beside them'.)
- Notice that sometimes a foot has three words of one syllable (mono-syllables), each of which must be given a fairly heavy stress. What does this suggest? (For example, look at 'Rain came down'.)

    Think of other **sound** effects used by Hardy in this poem, especially **alliteration** (look, for example, at lines 9 and 13), **assonance** of vowel sounds (often linked to the internal rhyme) and **repetition**.

Personification

Writers often use **personification** to give the impression of objects or natural forces having some kind of impact (which might be friendly or hostile) on the lives of human beings. (A particular form of this is what is called **pathetic fallacy**, in which a writer credits inanimate things with feelings.) In this poem, Hardy personifies the guns vividly. Study the 'human' words which he uses to describe the guns.

People's feelings

The poem has a large number of words to describe **feelings** and **attitudes** – sometimes the soldiers' but more particularly the women's. Underline the different words used, and think about the overall effect that these create.

Faith and trust

The poem contains a number of religious references, in the last three stanzas especially, with the words 'prayed', some 'Hand' (referring to a divine Hand) and 'in trust'. Think about how Hardy shows whether it was easy or difficult for the women to have faith, especially in the soldiers' return.

The women

In this poem, Hardy seems to enter into the thoughts of the women, by writing as though he is one of them – he says 'we' – and, in one place, using direct speech. This helps us to feel we, as readers, are present at the scene.

- In what particular ways does it help you to think about and respond to the poem?

15

Katherine Tynan (1861-1931)

Katherine Tynan was born in Dublin. She wrote more than 100 novels, five autobiographical volumes and many articles for newspapers, but she is best known for her poetry. Her friend, the famous Irish poet, W B Yeats, considered her to be an Irish Christina Rossetti (see the poems by Christina Rossetti 'A Birthday' and 'Remember', which are included in *Tracks*.) The strongest influences on her works were her Irish patriotism and religious upbringing.

Joining the Colours

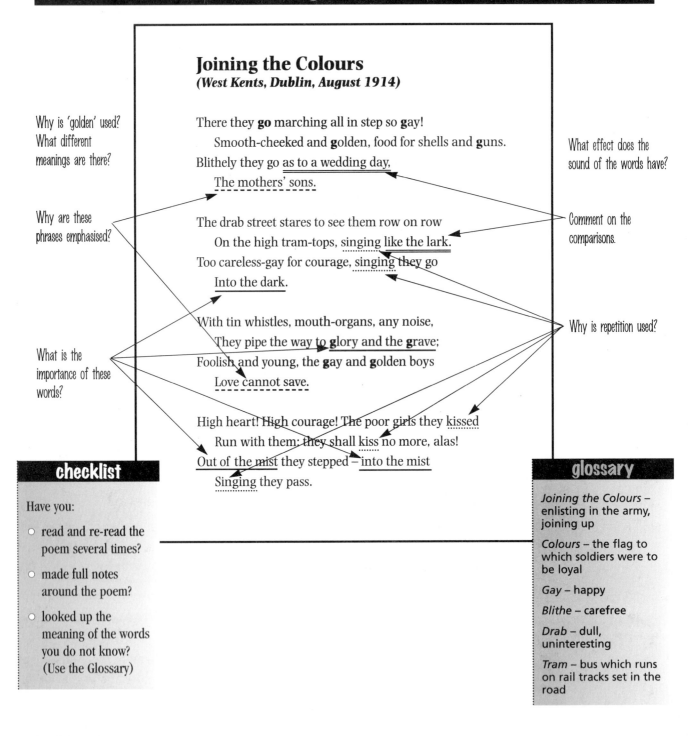

Joining the Colours
(West Kents, Dublin, August 1914)

Why is 'golden' used?
What different meanings are there?

What effect does the sound of the words have?

Why are these phrases emphasised?

Comment on the comparisons.

What is the importance of these words?

Why is repetition used?

There they **go** marching all in step so **g**ay!
   Smooth-cheeked and **g**olden, food for shells and **g**uns.
Blithely they go as to a wedding day,
   The mothers' sons.

The drab street stares to see them row on row
   On the high tram-tops, singing like the lark.
Too careless-gay for courage, singing they go
   Into the dark.

With tin whistles, mouth-organs, any noise,
   They pipe the way to **g**lory and the **g**rave;
Foolish and young, the **g**ay and **g**olden boys
   Love cannot save.

High heart! High courage! The poor girls they kissed
   Run with them; they shall kiss no more, alas!
Out of the mist they stepped – into the mist
   Singing they pass.

checklist

Have you:

○ read and re-read the poem several times?

○ made full notes around the poem?

○ looked up the meaning of the words you do not know? (Use the Glossary)

glossary

Joining the Colours – enlisting in the army, joining up

Colours – the flag to which soldiers were to be loyal

Gay – happy

Blithe – carefree

Drab – dull, uninteresting

Tram – bus which runs on rail tracks set in the road

When reading the poem, think about the following:
- What are the ideas, thoughts and feelings conveyed?
- What is interesting about how the poet conveys these?
- In what ways do you respond to the poem (language, style, tone, attitude)?

Here are some ideas to start you thinking.

The ideas in the poem

On a copy of the poem, underline in different colours all words in the poem related to:
- life and death
- the love and the emotions of those left behind
- the feelings of the soldiers.

Use these words to help you decide what the poet's attitudes are:
- to the soldiers
- to those left behind
- to war.

The language used

Think about the different ways in which the poet's language and poetic form create effects and add to the impact of the poem. You may wish to focus on such things as:
- choice of words
- use of alliteration
- personification
- imagery
- rhyme
- rhythm
- repetition
- exclamations
- contrasts
- structure.

Refer again to the annotated poem on page 16.

Exploring the senses

Put a ring round any words which convey:
- sight
- sound
- movement
- touch.

The scenes the poem creates

How clearly can you picture events and people? How does Tynan's language help you to imagine the scenes and the atmosphere and mood?

Comparisons

Which of the poems within the 'Front Lines' section of *Tracks* can you compare with this poem? Can you compare
- the scenes?
- the soldiers?
- the onlookers?
- the language?
- the attitudes of the poets?

Which is the most effective and why?

(Look back to pages 12 and 13 for suggestions on how to compare poems.)

Wilfred Owen (1893 – 1918)

Wilfred Owen was one of a number of young poets who wrote of their experiences in World War I, which was fought between 1914 and 1918. Owen died in action just seven days before the Armistice was declared on 11 November 1918. The bells which celebrated the end of the war were ringing in Shropshire, when the bell of the Owens' front door rang to announce the telegram with the news of Wilfred's death. He was awarded the Military Cross for bravery; he never saw his poems published.

In October 1915, Wilfred Owen joined the army ('joined the colours' of the British Artists' Rifles). During his time in the war he often wrote about his feelings towards war in letters to his mother. In January 1917, he led a platoon in the 5th (Reserve) Battalion of the Manchester Regiment into the battle of the Somme. He wrote about this experience to his mother: 'My dug-out held 25 men tight packed. Water filled it to a depth of 1 or 2 feet leaving only 4 feet in the air.'

In March he fell through a shell-hole into a cellar and was trapped in the dark for three days. This left him with a powerful sense of darkness and the Underworld, ideas which can be found in several of the poems. 'The Send-Off', for example, starts, ominously, with the word 'down'.

On the first of May, he was diagnosed as having neurasthenia, more commonly known as 'shell shock'. He was sent to recover in military hospitals, and at one of these, Craiglockhart, he met another poet, Siegfried Sassoon. Sassoon helped him to channel his memories of the battlefield, which were marked by obsessive nightmares, into poems. The encounters between Sassoon and Owen are graphically portrayed in the novel 'Regeneration', by Pat Barker. This is one of her three books (called a 'trilogy') about the war.

This account shows how Sassoon, the older man and more experienced writer, was able to make suggestions on the drafts of Owen's poems. Some of these changes can still be studied today, by looking at Owen's original manuscript versions and the crossings-out on them. (See 'Anthem for Doomed Youth', on pages 24 and 25, for an example.)

In late November 1917, Owen rejoined the 5th Manchesters in camp, and by June 1918 he was pronounced fit to resume military duties. He lived for barely five more months.

Owen's war poetry is a lasting memorial to those who experienced the horror of suffering and death in the trenches. In the introduction to his first book of poetry he wrote that 'The poetry is in the pity' and generations since World War I have been able to respond sympathetically to the images he created.

For the examination, you have to study only the five poems by Wilfred Owen which are listed in *Tracks*. However, if you become interested in Owen and would like to read more, you can find others in collections of poems (anthologies), including the poems 'Exposure', 'Strange Meeting', 'Mental Cases', 'Futility' and 'The Sentry'. These will enable you to carry out further exploration of Owen's themes and his treatment of war.

The Send-Off

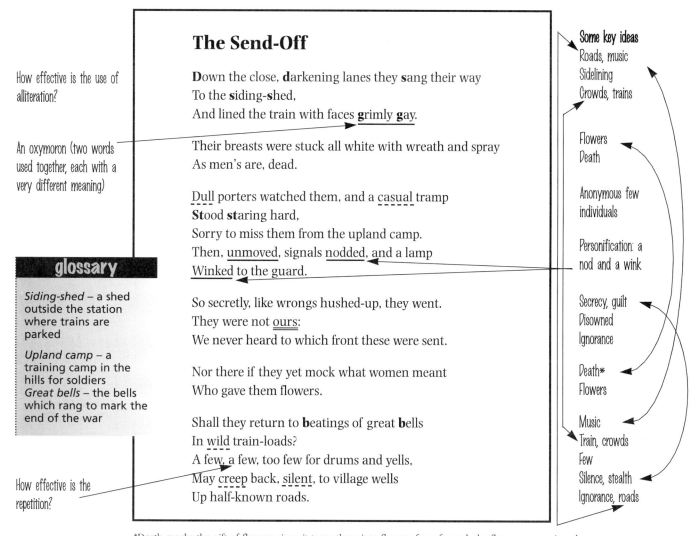

The Send-Off

How effective is the use of alliteration?

Down the close, **d**arkening lanes they **s**ang their way
To the **s**iding-**s**hed,
And lined the train with faces **g**rimly **g**ay.

An oxymoron (two words used together, each with a very different meaning)

Their breasts were stuck all white with wreath and spray
As men's are, dead.

Dull porters watched them, and a casual tramp
Stood **st**aring hard,
Sorry to miss them from the upland camp.
Then, unmoved, signals nodded, and a lamp
Winked to the guard.

So secretly, like wrongs hushed-up, they went.
They were not ours:
We never heard to which front these were sent.

Nor there if they yet mock what women meant
Who gave them flowers.

Shall they return to **b**eatings of great **b**ells
In wild train-loads?
A few, a few, too few for drums and yells,
May creep back, silent, to village wells
Up half-known roads.

How effective is the repetition?

glossary

Siding-shed – a shed outside the station where trains are parked

Upland camp – a training camp in the hills for soldiers
Great bells – the bells which rang to mark the end of the war

Some key ideas
Roads, music
Sidelining
Crowds, trains

Flowers
Death

Anonymous few
individuals

Personification: a
nod and a wink

Secrecy, guilt
Disowned
Ignorance

Death*
Flowers

Music
Train, crowds
Few
Silence, stealth
Ignorance, roads

*Death mocks the gift of flowers since it turns them into flowers for a funeral; the flowers were given by women; a wreath or garland of flowers can be used in celebration or it can mark a funeral; so can a spray.

• How does the way in which the poem is organised make use of the key ideas?

The poem is called 'The Send-Off', but it is also looking forward, imagining a 'homecoming'.
• How do these two scenes compare – the real one and the imagined one in the future?
• Is the mood similar or different?
• Is it a 'real' send-off? (Compare 'Joining the Colours' for the scene.) Why might the title seem ironic?
• Why does the poet give the impression of secrecy and guilt? What do these ideas tell you about Owen's feelings?

Think about the length of the words. In particular, look at the frequency of monosyllables (words with one syllable).

• Pick out the number of lines where all the words are monosyllables and those where there are only one or two words with two syllables.

Look particularly at the second and the second to last stanza.
• What do you notice about this pair of stanzas?
• Is there anywhere else in the poem where you feel that the build-up of monosyllabic words contributes to the mood and effect?
• How effective is this use?
• Study this poem alongside other Owen poems in the 'Front Lines' section of *Tracks*. Can you find similarities in:
  ○ his approach to the subject-matter
  ○ the themes
  ○ his use of images?

Inspection

Inspection

'You! What d'you mean by this?' I rapped.
'You dare come on parade like this?'
'Please, sir, it's—' ''Old yer mouth,' the sergeant snapped.
'I take 'is name, sir?'— 'Please, and then dismiss.'

Some days 'confined to camp' he got
For being 'dirty on parade'.
He told me afterwards, the damned spot
Was blood, his own. 'Well, blood is dirt,' I said.

'Blood's dirt,' he laughed, looking away
Far off to where his wound had bled
And almost merged for ever into clay.
'The world is washing out its stains,' he said.
'It doesn't like our cheeks so red.
Young blood's its great objection.
But when we're duly white-washed, being dead,
The race will bear Field-Marshal God's inspection.'

What is the effect of the sound of these verbs?

In 'Macbeth' (Shakespeare), Lady Macbeth cries 'Out, damned spot' when she is sleep-walking and trying to remove the blood of guilt from her hands.

This develops the idea of trying to wash away the evidence of guilt.

'White-washed': look at the different meanings.

glossary

Merged – mixed

Clay – soil; also, white clay is used for *white-washing* the webbing (canvas straps) on the soldiers' uniforms

Characters

There are three speaking characters in the poem:
the officer (**O**)
the sergeant (**S**)
the private (**P**)

- Make sure that you have worked out which of them says what.
- Label each of the speeches with the right letter in a chosen colour.
- If you wish, highlight each speech in the right colour, to make it easier to see which is which.
- What is your impression of each of the characters?
- What contrasts are there between them?

Think about:
○ different classes
○ different roles
○ different attitudes
○ how language is used to bring out the differences.

NB Make sure that you have found quotations from the text, and that these support the points you wish to make.
Do not just list quotations. Pick out **key words** and show the effect these have.

The importance of the title
- Why do you think the poet uses the word 'Inspection' in the title?
- What is the importance of inspections in a military organisation?
- How does the routine of inspections relate to the realities of war?
- In this poem, who is being 'inspected'? Is it only the common soldier?
- Why, at the end of the poem, does the poet describe God as 'Field Marshal God' and refer to God's 'inspection'?

Themes
Some of the themes which you can explore in this poem are:
- death
- guilt
- cleansing
- bureaucracy/following procedures
- the harsh realities of war
- military rank and discipline
- insensitivity to ordinary soldiers.

Colour coding
For each theme, underline any words or phrases that contribute to the ideas. You may wish to use colour coding as a way of marking the different themes. This should be helpful in enabling you to organise and select material to illustrate particular points.

Exploring the themes
Using this analysis, you should be in a position to consider **how** Owen uses the language to give the reader a clear idea of the poem's central concerns. Think about such points as:
- the use of **white** and **red**, or words which relate to these, and their **symbolic importance**;
- how different **registers** and **tones of voice** contribute to the themes. Consider the use of:
  - irony;
  - direct commands;
  - questioning;
  - formal language.
- use of **official military language**;
- use of **religious language and images**;
- cross-reference to **Shakespeare**.

Disabled

Disabled

Annotations (right margin, top to bottom):
- Time? Death?
- Appearance
- Sound/life
- Heightens his own isolation
- Metaphor – life
- Seems casual or deliberate
- Love, mystery
- Disgust
- Youth/age
- Life draining away
- Blood: a badge of victory – in sport
- Appearance
- Age
- Repetition
- Sport
- Regimented, confined Pity, not love
- Double meaning? Rhetorical questions

Annotations (left margin):
- Position of word in line
- Physical closeness: rejection
- Irony

He sat in a wheeled chair, waiting for dark,
And shivered in his **gh**astly suit of **g**rey,
Legless, sewn short at elbow. Through the park
Voices of boys rang saddening like a hymn,
Voices of play and pleasures after day,
Till gathering sleep had mothered them from him.

* * *

About this time Town used to swing so **g**ay
When **gl**ow-lamps budded in the light blue trees,
And **g**irls **gl**anced lovelier as the air **g**rew dim,–
In the old times, before he threw away his knees.
Now he will never feel again how slim
Girls' waists are, or how warm their subtle hands;
All of them touch him like some queer disease.

* * *

There was an artist silly for his face,
For it was younger than his youth, last year.
Now, he is old; his back will never brace;
He's lost his colour very far from here,
Poured it down shell-holes till the veins ran dry,
And half his lifetime lapsed in the hot race,
And **leap** of **pur**p**le sp**urted from his thigh.

* * *

One time he liked a blood-smear down his leg,
After the matches, carried shoulder-high.
It was after football, when he'd drunk a peg,
He thought he'd better join.–He wonders why.
Someone had said he'd look a god in kilts,
That's why; and may be, too, to please his Meg;
Aye, that was it, to please the giddy jilts
He asked to join. He didn't have to beg;
Smiling they wrote his lie; aged nineteen years.
Germans he scarcely thought of; all their guilt
And Austria's, did not move him. And no fears
Of Fear came yet. He thought of jewelled hilts
For daggers in plaid socks; of smart salutes;
And care of arms; and leave, and pay arrears;
Esprit de corps; and hints for young recruits.
And soon, he was drafted out with drums and cheers.

* * *

Some cheered him home, but not as crowds cheer Goal.
Only a solemn man who brought him fruits
Thanked him; and then enquired about his soul.

* * *

Now, he will spend a few sick years in institutes,
And do what things the rules consider wise,
And take whatever pity they may dole.
Tonight he noticed how the women's eyes
Passed from him to the strong men that were whole.
How cold and late it is! Why don't they come
And put him to bed? Why don't they come?

glossary

Peg – a drink

Giddy jilts – foolish young women

Hilts – handles

Plaid – tartan

Care of arms – looking after weapons

Leave – a period away from service

pay arrears – back pay owed to someone

Esprit de corps – community spirit

Drafted – sent to join a military unit

Dole – hand out

This powerful poem was written while Owen was in hospital. Here, he uses his detailed observations of young men whose lives had been drastically altered by the loss of limbs in battle, a common result of the use of shells to attack. Much of the strength of the poem lies in the skilful contrasts drawn. The title of the poem was changed from 'Why he joined' to 'Disabled', and the new title itself draws attention to one particular contrast: the man's state before and after the battle.

Contrasts

- life and death;
- able-bodied and disabled;
- heat and cold;
- war and sport;
- appearance and reality;
- day and night;
- freedom and confinement;
- love and loneliness;
- movement and immobility;
- hope and fear.

- Study the poem carefully and consider how these themes are presented. Note down examples of particular words and phrases which illustrate them.
- What other contrasting ideas can you find?

Joining up

You have looked at several poems which deal with young men 'joining up'. This poem describes the situation when one particular recruit signed on and his reasons for doing so.

- Why did he wish to join up?
- Do you feel that he acted with good reasons?
- What do you learn about the recruiting officers' attitudes?
- Why is his age important?

Language and sounds

Consider carefully the effect of the poet's choice of words and of their sounds. Think about, for example:

- rhythm
- rhyme
- alliteration
- similes
- metaphors
- tone.

Character

This poem gives a detailed picture of the young soldier who has been disabled.

- What impression do you have of him – before and afterwards? In what ways does the poet convey his views and affect our responses to the young man and his situation?

23

Anthem for Doomed Youth

We are now able to look more closely at 'Anthem for Doomed Youth', one of the two poems which were used on pages 12 and 13, as an introduction to how to compare and contrast poems. This is quoted in full again here, to make it easier to analyse. (The other poem used for that comparison is 'The Soldier', by Rupert Brooke, which is not included in the *Tracks* collection of war poetry, but it nevertheless offers the opportunity to practise working with two poems and shows very different attitudes to war.) The poem's title is immediately striking, because it uses, close together, two highly contrasting ideas: 'anthem' and 'doomed'. The word 'anthem' may seem an unusual choice, because the subject-matter of the poem is so obviously not that of most anthems, which are joyful hymns. It was suggested by the poet Siegfried Sassoon, when he was discussing the poem with Owen in Craiglockhart Hospital. Owen later wrote that this was 'just what he meant it to be'.

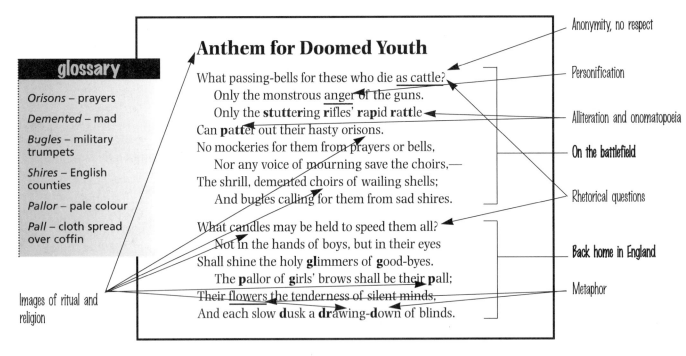

glossary

Orisons – prayers

Demented – mad

Bugles – military trumpets

Shires – English counties

Pallor – pale colour

Pall – cloth spread over coffin

Anthem for Doomed Youth

What passing-bells for these who die as cattle?
    Only the monstrous anger of the guns.
    Only the **st**u**tt**ering **r**ifles' **r**apid **r**attle
Can **patt**er out their hasty orisons.
No mockeries for them from prayers or bells,
    Nor any voice of mourning save the choirs,—
The shrill, demented choirs of wailing shells;
    And bugles calling for them from sad shires.

What candles may be held to speed them all?
    Not in the hands of boys, but in their eyes
Shall shine the holy **gl**immers of **g**ood-byes.
    The **p**allor of **g**irls' brows shall be their **p**all;
Their flowers the tenderness of silent minds,
And each slow **d**usk a **dr**awing-**d**own of blinds.

Labels around poem: Anonymity, no respect · Personification · Alliteration and onomatopoeia · On the battlefield · Rhetorical questions · Back home in England · Metaphor · Images of ritual and religion

The Sonnet

The sonnet form has been popular in many periods of poetry, and was greatly used by William Shakespeare. Wilfred Owen found its concise and economic structure a suitable form for some of his most hard-hitting poems, and it was also, as we have seen (pages 12 and 13), the form used by Rupert Brooke in 'The Soldier'.

Tasks

Look closely at the organisation of 'Anthem for Doomed Youth', thinking about how Owen has used the sonnet form to gain his effect. You should consider:

○ the *links* and *contrasts* between the two sections, the **octave** (the first eight lines) and the **sestet** (the final six). Note the use of rhetorical questions, the changes in tone and situation, but also the continuity of theme between the two parts;

○ the *rhythm*: Owen uses the **iambic pentameter**, with its basic pattern of unstressed and stressed syllables: **x/ x/ x/ x/ x/**. This rhythm has a natural, flowing effect, often close to normal speech patterns, but can occasionally be altered slightly to give a particular emphasis, for example a heavier start to the line;

○ the way in which the *images* used (especially those of religion, ritual and music/sound) run like threads through the poem and hold it together;

○ the *themes* with which Owen is concerned, and how these relate to other of his poems which you have studied;

○ the *tone of voice* which the poem adopts, and the effect of this.

The drafting of the poem

When discussing the poem, Sassoon made a number of suggestions for changes to the original draft which Wilfred Owen showed him, especially at the start of the poem. In her First World War novel, 'Regeneration', Pat Barker imagines the conversations between Sassoon and Owen which led to these changes. The manuscript version, with Sassoon's suggested changes on it, still exists, and gives a fascinating insight into how poets work on finding exactly the right word. The final version of the first two lines is printed below, and under each line are the words which Owen included in the earlier draft:

What passing-bells for these who die as cattle?
minute-bells   *so fast?*
        Only the monstrous anger of the guns.
            solemn   *our*

- What do you feel about the changes between the original and the final version?
- Which words do you find particularly effective, and why?

A Revision Guide to the Use of Quotations in Poetry Answers, Using 'Anthem for Doomed Youth' as an Example

Here are **ten pointers** which should help to ensure success in your answers:

1 Include well-chosen quotations, making sure that they support your critical points.
2 Remember the sequence: **critical point: illustration: comment**.
3 Keep quotations brief – that is, restrict yourself to the **key**, **relevant** words or phrases.
4 It is unlikely that a quotation which is more than **two lines long** will be entirely relevant.
5 Mark all quotations clearly by placing them inside **quotation marks**.
6 Wherever possible, include the quotation within your own sentence structure.
7 Do not list quotations: use them.
8 Introductory comments which identify the poet's technique will enable you to make the most of your examples, e.g.: 'the poet uses repetition skilfully in the words....'
9 Do not just give the names or number of technical features or devices. Never simply say, for example: 'There are four similes in this poem....'
10 Keep to the positive – do not refer to what is not there, for example: 'There is no alliteration in this poem'. There is no rule which states that all poems must include certain devices.

Using quotations – some examples
The examples which follow suggest some ways of working quotations into your sentences, using 'Anthem for Doomed Youth' as an illustration.

Sound: *Owen's use of alliteration and onomatopoeia in the phrase 'stuttering rifles' rapid rattle' gives a horrifying sense of the sound of being under continual gunfire.*

Imagery: *Owen imagines that, in place of funeral flowers, the dead will be remembered in 'the tenderness of quiet minds'. Flowers fade rapidly, but the loved ones of the dead will keep them alive in their tender thoughts.*

Repetition: *Owen's use of the repetition of 'choirs' is particularly striking. The first mention makes the reader think of a real choir at a typical funeral. However, when this word is repeated in the phrase 'the shrill demented choirs of wailing shells' we see that there will be no songs of remembrance, only the incessant, harsh sounds of battle.*

Tone: *The sad, haunting notes of 'bugles calling for them from sad shires' are echoed in the final line of the whole poem. The 'drawing-down of blinds', a traditional sign of mourning in households stricken with death, is repeated, metaphorically, each day at nightfall.*

Attitude: *The poet sets out his bitterness at the young soldiers' deaths, already indicated in the ironic title, by using the simile 'these who die as cattle' to give a strong sense of the futility of war.*

Dulce et Decorum Est

Dulce et Decorum Est

Bent double, like old beggars under sacks,
Knock-kneed, coughing like hags, we cursed through sludge,
Till on the haunting flares we turned our backs,
And towards our distant rest began to trudge.
Men marched asleep. Many had lost their boots,
But limped on, blood-shod. All went lame, all blind;
Drunk with fatigue; deaf even to the hoots
Of gas-shells dropping softly behind.

Gas! Gas! Quick, boys!—An ecstasy of fumbling,
Fitting the clumsy helmets just in time,
But someone still was yelling out and stumbling
And floundering like a man in fire or lime.—
Dim through the misty panes and thick green light,
As under a green sea, I saw him drowning.

In all my dreams before my helpless sight
He plunges at me, guttering, choking, drowning.

If in some smothering dreams, you too could pace
Behind the wagon that we flung him in,
And watch the white eyes writhing in his face,
His hanging face, like a devil's sick of sin;
If you could hear, at every jolt, the blood
Come gargling from the froth-corrupted lungs,
Bitter as the cud
Of vile, incurable sores on innocent tongues,—
My friend, you would not tell with such high zest
To children ardent for some desperate glory,
The old Lie: Dulce et decorum est
Pro patria mori.

Annotations (right margin)

Why does Owen start his poem with these images?

Note the frequent use of verbs ending in -ing (present participles)

'Dreams' is repeated: why is this?

What is the effect of the direct address to the readers?

'Cud' is the half-digested food that cattle chew again: why does Owen use this word here?

glossary

Sludge – mud

Blood-shod – feet covered with blood

Fatigue – exhaustion

Ecstasy – frenzy

Lime – a substance which burns

Panes – windows in gas masks

Guttering – pouring down (with blood)

Writhing – twisting in pain

Ardent – desiring (passionately)

The Latin words which give this poem its title and its last two lines come from the Roman poet Horace, who wrote in the first century BC. In Owen's day, many educated people knew the ancient Roman authors well, and quoting from them was not unusual, partly as a sign of one's education. This particular phrase, meaning 'It is sweet and fitting to die for one's country', became almost a motto, used to support patriotic statements about the war. It is interesting to note that in a poem which he wrote around the start of the war, called 'The Ballad of Peace and War', Wilfred Owen himself had supported this idea:

Oh it is sweet and it is meet
To live in peace with others
But sweeter still and far more meet
To die in war with brothers.

- Compare the tone of the last four lines of 'Dulce et Decorum Est' with the above stanza.
- What do you learn from this comparison about the changes in Owen's attitude towards the war?
  You should note that 'Dulce et Decorum Est' was written three years later, in 1917.

Key words and phrases

Using your chosen system for marking the text (for example, underlining, highlighting or colour coding), pick out from the poem examples of the following:

- imagery (eg, similes, metaphors): think about the subjects from which the images are drawn;
- effects of sound;
- rhythmic effects;
- words related to colour;
- different types of movement/travel;
- unusually long or short sentences: consider the effect of these;
- words which paint particularly striking pictures.

- **Think about how effective the key words and phrases which you have found are in contributing to your understanding of the poem.**

Themes

Look carefully at the organisation into different stanzas, and see how each of these sets out and develops the central themes of the poem. Note down what these themes are and any key words which emphasise them.

Tone of voice and mood

Think about the tone of voice and mood the poet communicates at different points in the poem:

- **To what extent do any of the following words capture these? (Give examples to illustrate this.)**
- **Can you think of other suitable words to describe the tone and mood?**

IRONIC DESPERATE	DRAMATIC		SHOCKED	HORRIFIED
BITTER	SORROWFUL	SAVAGE		DETACHED
HAUNTING			DISILLUSIONED	SYMPATHETIC

Gas

This poem is one of the most famous and frequently read of Owen's war poems.

- Why do you think it is so well-known?
- Does it deserve its fame?
- What does it make you feel about war?
- How do your feelings compare with Owen's?
- What particular aspects of the war provide the focus for Owen's writing here?
- How does Owen make you aware that he is personally involved in the events he describes?

In your reading of *Tracks*, you will find other passages dealing with the effects of the use of gas, especially chlorine or mustard gas. Think about the ways in which the different writers treat this subject.

- **Are there ways in which either the prose passages or this poem make the effects described seem particularly vivid or horrifying? Compare this view of warfare in the First World War with those of other wars described in poems or prose in the *Tracks* selection.**

Alan Ross (1922 –)

Alan Ross joined the Royal Navy as an ordinary seaman on convoys to Russia. He later served in the Intelligence section with destroyer flotillas. In 1946, he joined naval staff in West Germany. 'Something of the Sea', written in 1954, drew on his naval experiences.

Night Patrol

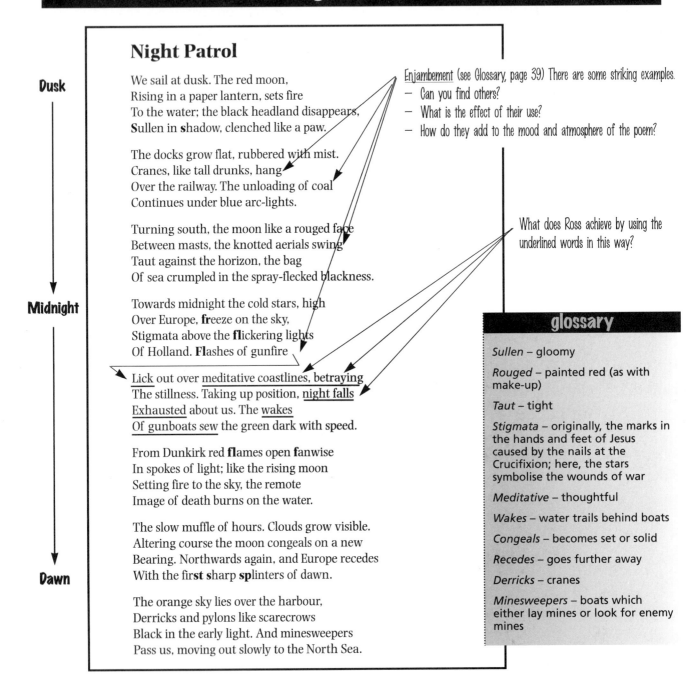

Dusk

Night Patrol

We sail at dusk. The red moon,
Rising in a paper lantern, sets fire
To the water; the black headland disappears,
Sullen in **s**hadow, clenched like a paw.

The docks grow flat, rubbered with mist.
Cranes, like tall drunks, hang
Over the railway. The unloading of coal
Continues under blue arc-lights.

Turning south, the moon like a rouged face
Between masts, the knotted aerials swing
Taut against the horizon, the bag
Of sea crumpled in the spray-flecked blackness.

Midnight

Towards midnight the cold stars, high
Over Europe, **f**reeze on the sky,
Stigmata above the **fl**ickering lights
Of Holland. **Fl**ashes of gunfire

Lick out over meditative coastlines, betraying
The stillness. Taking up position, night falls
Exhausted about us. The wakes
Of gunboats sew the green dark with speed.

From Dunkirk red **fl**ames open **f**anwise
In spokes of light; like the rising moon
Setting fire to the sky, the remote
Image of death burns on the water.

The slow muffle of hours. Clouds grow visible.
Altering course the moon congeals on a new
Bearing. Northwards again, and Europe recedes
With the fir**st** **s**harp **sp**linters of dawn.

Dawn

The orange sky lies over the harbour,
Derricks and pylons like scarecrows
Black in the early light. And minesweepers
Pass us, moving out slowly to the North Sea.

Enjambement (see Glossary, page 39) There are some striking examples.
– Can you find others?
– What is the effect of their use?
– How do they add to the mood and atmosphere of the poem?

What does Ross achieve by using the underlined words in this way?

glossary

Sullen – gloomy

Rouged – painted red (as with make-up)

Taut – tight

Stigmata – originally, the marks in the hands and feet of Jesus caused by the nails at the Crucifixion; here, the stars symbolise the wounds of war

Meditative – thoughtful

Wakes – water trails behind boats

Congeals – becomes set or solid

Recedes – goes further away

Derricks – cranes

Minesweepers – boats which either lay mines or look for enemy mines

Dunkirk was the coastal town in France from which large numbers of Allied soldiers were forced to retreat from the advancing German troops. Large and small boats mounted a rescue operation which successfully brought 300,000 of these troops safely back to England. These determined and often heroic efforts led to the expression 'the Dunkirk spirit' to refer to the defiance shown against the Germans, at a time when Britain faced the constant threat of invasion. (See also the passage 'Evacuees in Thanet', in *Tracks*.)

The title

As is often the case in the poems you have studied, the title gives an indication of what the poem is about. Think about what the purpose of such a patrol was in the Second World War.

- What were the patrol boats looking for?
- What feelings would the men on the boat have experienced?
- How does the landscape reflect the mood?

The passage of time

This poem deals with a series of events and scenes over a clearly-stated period of time. There are three particular times mentioned:

Dusk   **Midnight**   **Dawn**

On a sheet of paper, note down for each of these three points all that the poet enables you to find out about the scene, paying attention both to the appearance of the sky and sea and to any places mentioned.

- What do you also discover about the changes taking place between dusk and midnight and between midnight and dawn?

War and peace

In some ways this seems to be a fairly peaceful scene, since there is no violent action such as that described by Wilfred Owen in 'Dulce et Decorum Est'. However, the poet gives a number of clues that suggest that everything is not really so calm.

- What are these clues?
- How do they suggest an atmosphere of war?
- How would you describe this atmosphere?

Use of colour

The poet paints the scenes by using a number of words which help the reader to 'see' what is going on. In particular, there are many colour words and ideas of light and darkness.

- Highlight or underline all words which refer to particular colours.
- Using a different way of marking the words, pick out those which convey the ideas of light or darkness.
- Apart from helping to give a visual picture, what do these words symbolise or represent in the poem?

Imagery

Find examples of the following forms of imagery and discuss with a friend what you have found, and what you think of these images:

- similes
- metaphors
- personification
- contrasts: heat/cold; land/water

Movement

Go through the poem carefully, finding all the verbs that describe movement.

- Who or what in each case is moving, and where is the movement leading?
- What differences are there in the speed of movement?
- What, in the poem, is described as *not* moving, and what effect does this have?

Elizabeth Jennings (1926 –)

Elizabeth Jennings started to write poems in her early teens. She spent some time working in libraries and in publishing, before becoming a lecturer and then a freelance writer. In 1955, her book 'A Way of Looking' won the Somerset Maugham Award. She has continued to write a large number of works, which often offer a deep exploration of emotions, and has published several collections of poems. She feels that 'a deeply held belief is bound to influence... all you write'. She was 13 when the Second World War broke out. In this poem she recaptures her memories and feelings, as a child at that time, about the outbreak of war, as she tried to relate the announcement to what she had previously learnt about war.

The Second World War

The Second World War

The voice said 'We are at War'
And I was afraid, for I did not know what this meant.
My sister and I ran to our friends next door
As if they could help. History was lessons learnt
   With ancient dates, but here

Was something utterly new,
The radio, called the wireless then, had said
That the country would have to be brave. There was much to do
And I remember that night as I lay in bed
   I thought of soldiers who

Had stood on our nursery floor
Holding guns, on guard and stiff. But war meant blood
Shed over battle-fields. Cavalry galloping. War
On that September Sunday made us feel frightened
   Of what our world waited for.

Language

For many of the poems in the 'Front Lines' selection in *Tracks*, a glossary has been included, to help with the explanation of more unusual words.

- Why is a glossary unnecessary with this particular poem?
- What is Elizabeth Jennings hoping to suggest by using vocabulary of this kind?

Look closely at the words and phrases underlined in the text above and think about their meaning in the poem:

- *The voice* (line 1). What voice is this? What is the effect of referring to 'the voice' in this way?

- *As if they could help* (line 4). How old do you think these friends are? How do the words suggest that this is a child's way of reacting to the news?
- *There was much to do* (line 8). What kinds of thing would ordinary people have had to do to prepare for the war?
- *Cavalry galloping* (line 12). What kind of war does Elizabeth Jennings seem to have in mind here?
- *Our world* (line 15). What do you think this world is for Elizabeth Jennings – her family's world, her country, the whole world?

The form of the poem

Look closely at how the poem is organised.

You should note in particular:

- ○ stanzas
- ○ rhyme scheme
- ○ line length
- ○ enjambement
- ○ rhythm.

- How does the organisation of the poem help to convey the idea that these are the thoughts and feelings of a child?

Exploring the poem

Think about the following questions:

History and education

- Why does the writer make a contrast between hearing the announcement of war and the history she had learnt at school?
- How does the poem make it clear that the writer does not have a clear idea of what the Second World War would be like?

Games and reality

- Why does the writer refer to the toy soldiers she used to play with?
- How do these toy soldiers differ from real soldiers and war, and why is this contrast so important?

Memories and emotions

- How do we know from the poem that the writer is looking back to these events over quite a long period?
- People can be afraid of what they do not know or understand, as well as what they do know about. Which kind of fear is it that Elizabeth Jennings feels?

Remember to find examples and quotations which will support your ideas.

Further tasks

- If war were announced today, how would we first hear about it? With a friend or in a group, discuss or write about the announcement and your reactions to it.
- Elizabeth Jennings remembers playing with toy soldiers. What part do war games (eg. board or computer games) play in our own society? Why are they so popular?

Carol Ann Duffy (1955 –)

Carol Ann Duffy was born in Glasgow, Scotland. She published her first volume of poetry even before she went to university. She won a series of awards and writers' fellowships, and she became a 'writer in residence', working in East London schools. Her poems deal with challenging themes and she is noted for her power to shock through the use of language and her thought-provoking and sometimes unusual subject-matter. Her poem 'War Photographer' draws on her close friendship with Don McCullin, one of the best-known of all war photographers, whose pictures of modern-day wars, especially the Vietnam War, have presented us with some of the most powerful and dramatic images of the human suffering which war can cause.

War Photographer

War Photographer

In his darkroom he is finally <u>alone</u>
with <u>spools of suffering</u> set out in <u>ordered rows</u>.
The only light is red and softly glows,
as though this were a church and he
a priest preparing to intone a Mass.
<u>Belfast. Beirut. Phnom Penh. All flesh is grass</u>.

He has a job to do. Solutions slop in trays
beneath his hands which did not tremble then
though seem to now. <u>Rural England</u>. Home again
to <u>ordinary pain</u> which <u>simple weather</u> can dispel,
to fields which don't explode beneath the feet
of running children in a <u>nightmare heat</u>.

Something is happening. A stranger's features
faintly start to twist before his eyes,
a <u>half-formed ghost</u>. He remembers the cries
of this man's wife, how he sought approval
without words to do what someone must
<u>and how the blood stained into foreign dust</u>.

A hundred agonies in black-and-white
from which his editor will pick out five or six
for Sunday's supplement. The reader's eyeballs <u>prick</u>
<u>with tears between the bath and pre-lunch beers</u>.
From the aeroplane he stares impassively at where
he earns his living and <u>they do not care</u>.

checklist

○ Look closely at the importance of the underlined words and phrases.

○ Note the effect of the use of words relating to sight and colour.

○ Think about the links between the two lines indicated.

glossary

Spools – rolls of film

Intone – chant

Dispel – remove

Impassively – without expression or feeling

The structure of the poem
- Go through the poem, working out the rhyme scheme which is used. Note carefully which lines in each stanza rhyme with each other. Is there a regular pattern?
- What does Duffy highlight with the particular words which she chooses for her rhymes?
- *Tears… . beers* (line 22): what is the effect of this use of internal rhyme?

- For each stanza, look at what is said about places. How important are the changes of scene in the poem's structure?
- Look at the stages of development of the photographs within the structure of the poem.

Use of places

You have just looked at places and their importance in the poem's structure. Notice that three particular cities are listed at the end of the first stanza:

Belfast   Beirut   Phnom Penh

- For each of these, find out as much as you can about their importance in recent wars (in Northern Ireland, Lebanon and Cambodia).

You may be able to look at war photographs which give a vivid impression of life in these cities in time of war, and the effect on the people and buildings. Think about other cities of which you have heard or read, which have suffered particularly from war damage. (Some of the prose passages you will be studying in *Tracks* will offer examples.)

The poem begins with the photographer enclosed in a darkroom and ends with him in an aeroplane, looking down on the world. In between, he goes, in his memories, to battlefields in far countries.
- What are his reactions to these places?
- In what ways does the poem contrast England with countries torn by war?
- Contrasts between home and abroad are found in other war poems. Can you find examples of this from the poems you have studied in *Tracks*, and what contrasts are made in these?

Use of religious imagery

In the first stanza, the photographer is compared to a priest in a church.
- What points do you think the poet is trying to emphasise in this comparison?
- The sentence 'All flesh is grass' is taken from the Bible, meaning that life fades and dies, like grass. Why do you think this sentence is placed next to the names of the three cities?

Two ways of recording the events of war

The war photographer

The work of a war photographer is difficult and can attract strong feelings, including criticism.
- Underline any words or phrases in this poem which show how he feels about this work. Why do you think he does such a job?

The poet

In this poem Carol Ann Duffy comments that the photographer's record of war is one made 'without words' (line 17).
- How does the poet use language to bring the pictures of war to life?
- In what ways does a photograph differ from a picture in words?
- What war photographs, poems or prose passages have made a strong impression on you?

Study the attitudes of the Sunday supplement readers who are imagined in the last stanza of the poem.
- How does the photographer feel about their reactions?
- How does the poet's choice of language show their attitude?
- Which of the following words best describe this attitude?

     caring   apathetic
     appalled   moved
     indifferent

- What is the tone of the poet in describing the way in which these people react?

'Front Lines' Poetry: Specimen Questions: Question 1 (2F/4H)

The following are examples to help you to revise and plan your answers. They are intended to assist with preparation for both tiers.

Hardy — ***The Going of the Battery***
- What are the feelings of the women about their men going to war? Give examples from the text.
- How does Hardy use the sound of this poem to emphasise meaning and ideas? Give examples.

Tynan — ***Joining the Colours***
- How important are sound and movement in the effectiveness of this poem?
- The poem is called 'Joining the Colours'. How does the presentation of events show whether Tynan's attitude towards the war is one of patriotism?

Owen — ***The Send-Off***
- What impression of war does this poem create? Give examples from the text.
- How does the language used by Owen contribute to the effectiveness of the poem? Illustrate your answer by close reference to the text.

Dulce et Decorum Est
- In what ways does Owen's language suggest the horror of the experience of a gas attack? Refer closely to the text.
- How does this poem show Owen's disillusionment with patriotic ideas? Support your answer from the text.

Inspection
- How effective are the different voices in the poem? Refer closely to the text.
- How does Owen use imagery in this poem to express his views on military routine? Support your answer from the text.

Anthem for Doomed Youth
- From this poem, analyse fully the way in which Owen explores his thoughts and feelings about the First World War. Give examples.
- How does the use of imagery in this poem convey the sadness of the soldiers' deaths? Use the text to support your ideas.

Disabled
- To what extent does this poem make you feel sympathy for the disabled soldier? Support your answer with examples from the text.
- Discuss, with close reference to the text, the importance of the contrasts between past and present in this poem.

Ross — ***Night Patrol***
- Discuss the effectiveness of the use of colour in creating the scene of the 'Night Patrol'.
- In what ways does the poem make you feel that those on the patrol have an important mission to perform? Refer closely to the text.

Jennings — ***The Second World War***
- How does the poet enable you to understand a child's reaction to the outbreak of war? Give examples to support your views.
- How far have the girl's previous experiences prepared her for the realities of war? Refer closely to references in the text.

Duffy — ***The War Photographer***
- How does the poet's use of language reveal the attitudes of the photographer?
- How effective is the use of contrast within the poem? Support your answer with reference to the text.

Model answers for 'Front Lines' poetry selection

On the previous page, there are a number of specimen examination questions, of the kind set for Question 1 on both Paper 2F and Paper 4H. You may wish to use these in the following three ways:

1 Take five minutes to plan an answer, using the relevant poem from *Tracks*.
2 Choose any one question and make a list of the quotations and references you would use in your answer; write notes on how you would comment on these.
3 Practise writing one or more questions to time, allowing yourself no more than 40 minutes for planning and writing.

NB For revision purposes, these questions are all set on individual poems, but you should remember that sometimes the examination may ask you to compare your ideas on two poems, as is done on pages 12 and 13.

Question 1

Remember the assessment objectives for this question. They are:

i) Main Assessment Objective: to develop and sustain interpretation of text;

ii) Supporting Assessment Objectives:
- to read with insight and engagement;
- to make appropriate reference to the text.

A good answer will show
- a personal response to the situations, characters and language;
- the ability to select and use examples to support your views.

You should not just list a large number of technical features or facts in your answer. You should look closely at all **key words** in the question and in the poem before starting your answer.

Example 1: The Going Of The Battery (Hardy)

- **What are the feelings of the women about their men going to war? Give examples from the text.**

Note the key words in the question: **feelings, women, men, war, examples**.
- The question is about the **women's feelings**, not the men's;
- You must support your views by **examples** from the poem.

Model Answer

This is not intended to be an 'ideal' answer, but to illustrate the approach looked for.

The title itself gives an immediate idea, in the words 'Wives' Lament', that the poem is about a distressing occasion. Hardy wrote the poem from the standpoint of the women who were left behind when their husbands went to South Africa to fight in the Boer War.

The women's feelings are stated strongly in the first line, with the words 'sad enough, weak enough, mad enough'. The emphatic repetition of 'enough' underlines the strength of the feelings: they were 'sad' at the thought of their husbands' departure, but they also felt 'weak', perhaps at the idea of having to live without them. They also believed they must have been 'mad' first of all to choose soldiers as husbands and secondly to let them go to war.

Despite these feelings, they were loyal to their men and fearlessly ('unblenchingly') walked along with them. The dactylic rhythm gives an impression of their regular steps as they sought to keep up with their marching husbands — you can almost hear them squelching through the mud.

The frightening sight of the mounted guns, personified by the poet so that they are like great monsters looking up to the sky, helps to bring home to them how serious the situation is. They begin to go through differing emotions. They are desperate for a final kiss, but are pale with anxiety: the faint, eerie gaslight brings out this pallor. They plead with the soldiers not to take unnecessary risks. This farewell is agonising for them, and their faces are now drenched with tears: 'blinded these eyes of ours'. They are sobbing bitterly. Finally, the soldiers depart, and the women have to retrace their steps, no longer 'unblenchingly': there is no point in 'putting on a brave face' any more, and their true feelings start to come out.

The poem now focuses on how the women are thinking and feeling after the men have left. They are all praying for their husbands' protection, but some now start to fear the worst and become pessimistic about the future: 'Nevermore will they come'. However, others try to be more positive, refusing to give in to such depressing thoughts: 'O it was wrong!'. They pray that, sooner or later, they will return, under some divine guidance.

Hardy shows clearly that the women do not find it easy, as the last stanza underlines. However hard the women may try to cling to belief, there are times (especially at night) when they will need all their faith and trust to shake off the 'voices' of doubt which recur ('haunting us, daunting us, taunting us'). Yet the final voice is one with a hard-fought optimism, giving the women the inner strength they need to carry them through the hard times ahead. Throughout the poem, Hardy has succeeded in capturing the drama of the situation and the intensity of the women's feelings by his skilful and evocative use of language.

Example 2: Inspection (Owen)

- **How does Owen use imagery in this poem to express his views on military routine? Support your answer from the text.**

Note the key words in the question: **imagery**, **views**, **military routine**.

Model Answer

In the poem 'Inspection', even the title conveys the image of strict military procedures. We think of soldiers cleaning boots, checking uniforms and making sure that all equipment is in good working order. We imagine the soldiers lined up in their rows on the parade ground, hoping that all is correct when the inspecting officer looks over them.

The officer's first words, therefore, emphasise the differences between the ranks. The officer's language is impersonal: 'You! What d'you mean by this?'. This reveals that the officer is angry that all is not perfect. Even the sergeant does not allow the soldier to finish his explanation.

The very strict hierarchy is clear, and there is a strong contrast in how the three men speak. The soldier and the sergeant call the officer 'sir'. The only difference is that the sergeant is asked 'please'. Both the officer and the sergeant speak in terse monosyllables. There words are shot out: 'rapped' and 'snapped'.

The second stanza gradually reveals that the soldier was found to be 'dirty on parade'. This is the type of cold, military phrase which would be used on a charge sheet, just as 'confined to camp' would be used to refer to the punishment given to someone who had failed an inspection or committed any other crime against routine.

The image of dirt is central to the poem. There is a cross-reference to Lady Macbeth's 'damned spot', which is another kind of dirt. This also links closely to the first reference to blood, which forms the second image. It is not the blood of a murderer, as in 'Macbeth', but the soldier's own blood, caused by a wound in battle. It is ironic that the blood was shed or 'earned' by his military duties. The inspection does not credit this fact at all. Life and death through service in war are unimportant, whereas the trivial aspects of a routine military inspection are all-important. 'Well, blood is dirt' shows that the officer is preoccupied with routine and does not see that the soldier could have died.

The soldier reflects on the moments on the battlefield when 'his wound had bled and almost merged forever into clay'. This is a powerful image: the clay is the earth but clay can also be 'white' and used to whiten the webbing of a soldier's uniform for inspection.

The graphic line, 'The world is washing out its stains' links with 'white-washing' and reminds us of the need to be cleansed from guilt. If 'the world' is involved in this process, this suggests that the whole earth is collectively guilty. In the final line, the suggestion is made that 'Field Marshal God' will inspect the world. Owen ironically questions whether the human race can in fact 'bear' such an inspection when life has been washed away by death.

To end with a reference to an inspection by God shows how Owen uses the poem to comment on the superficial preoccupation with organisation and procedure at the expense of young lives in war-time.

Example 3: Disabled (Owen)

- **To what extent does this poem make you feel sympathy for the disabled soldier? Support your answer with examples from the text.**

Note the key words in the question: **sympathy**, **disabled soldier**, **examples**.

Model Answer

'Disabled' is a moving portrait of a young soldier who has had his limbs — both legs and arms — blown away in war. Owen does not try to sentimentalise his situation. This was a young man who had had a life full of promise, but now is a figure of helplessness, contrasted sharply with the able-bodied.

At the start of the poem, we are presented with the image of his wheelchair, and the phrase 'waiting for death' suggests strongly that there is nothing left in his life. His clothes — 'a ghastly suit of grey' — emphasise that all colour has gone from his life; his sleeves are 'sewn short at the elbow'. There is a touching contrast between those who are playing in the park and the young, disabled soldier who has lost all of his youth and mobility. The voices of those in the park are happy, yet to the soldier they seem 'saddening like a hymn', because they remind him of his changed life. This idea creates sympathy for him, and this becomes even stronger as we see the boys return home to sleep and to their mothers' arms, while he is left isolated and unloved.

We feel a strong sense that he had once been a young, handsome man, who could remember the warmth of love and girls. Now, however, he is cut off from this. Owen makes it seem as though the loss of limbs was almost a casual, reckless act: 'he threw away his knees'. Our sympathy is aroused by the fact that he no longer feels any warm, sensuous touches; if anyone touches him, it is as though he has 'some queer disease'. His disability has dehumanised him in other people's eyes.

Our view of the soldier is given even greater impact by the references to him as a youthful artist's model: 'there was an artist silly for his face'. Now, he has been totally transformed from a state of fitness, from being someone who would look 'a god in kilts', to a man in a crippled, deformed condition.

Further sympathy is created by the contrast between his present state, with its horrific wounds, and the picture we have of the young man as an athlete. A keen footballer, he had been proud of his trophy, 'a blood-smear down his leg'. His life was not threatened, but it proved that he had been in a 'battle'. This leads into reflections on why he became a soldier. The reader is able to see the links between the competitive nature of a young sportsman and the desire to fight for one's own country. When playing football he was proud to wear the team colours, not least because he was admired by the women, and he was equally keen to wear the flattering kilt. The fact that he was under-age was no obstacle, to him or to the recruiting officers.

His rather naïve reasons for joining up underline the pathos, since he was not even feeling a strong patriotic sense of duty. We realise that he was sucked into war without realising or under-standing fully what he was letting himself in for. He was filled with the glamour of the situation. The 'drums and cheers' may have accompanied him when he was 'drafted out', but the mood was very different when the crowds cheered him home: 'not as crowds cheer Goal'. There is no real sense of a nation's gratitude for a war hero who has sacrificed so much: the irony is sensed in the man who 'thanked him' and then 'enquired about his soul', simply out of a sense of religious duty.

The poem ends with the emptiness of his present life and with the chilling future that awaits him. This is powerfully shown in the monosyllables of 'Now he will spend a few sick years'. The reader feels sympathy for him when the girls who used to express pride in his appearance now prefer 'strong men that were whole'.

The final lines create a stark, forlorn figure waiting for death. His plight arouses our pity, because through him we see a whole generation cruelly affected by war and abandoned by those at home.

Example 4: War Photographer (Duffy)

- **How does the poet's use of language reveal the attitudes of the photographer?**

Note the key words in the question: **language**, **attitudes**.

Model Answer

Carol Ann Duffy's poem, 'War Photographer', captures realistically the thoughts and attitudes of the central figure, the photographer.

The first thing we learn is that he is 'finally alone'. In his working life, he is constantly surrounded by people in the thick of dramatic events. Now, at last, he is in his quiet darkroom, in the process of turning the mass of images of war, 'spools of suffering set out in ordered rows', into publishable prints. In this isolation, he becomes almost a different person, in a world of his own. The comparison with the priest, 'as though this were a church and he a priest preparing to intone a Mass', emphasises the ritual elements of his activities. We can imagine him going through a catalogue of cities – 'Belfast. Beirut. Phnom Penh' – like the priest chanting biblical phrases: 'All flesh is grass'.

However, he is motivated by the fact that, in Duffy's direct phrase, 'he has a job to do'. This sentence underlines that he must get on with it, in just the same way that he did when he was out in the battlefields. It is ironic that he is more afraid now – afraid, presumably, that the pictures will not capture the events convincingly enough – than he had been when actually taking the photographs, surrounded by 'running children in a nightmare heat'. Now he is in 'Rural England', with 'fields that don't explode', and he feels an 'ordinary pain': the everyday routine is more difficult to bear than the minefields.

These attitudes of the war photographer are reinforced by Duffy's language when she presents the images on the film starting to become recognisable ('A stranger's features faintly start to twist before his eyes'), and bringing back the memories. The photographer recalls not just the horror of the scene and the 'half-formed ghost', but also the difficult discussions he had to undertake with the man's wife in order to get permission to take the photographs. He remains rather matter-of-fact, and he still feels that 'he has a job to do'. However, Duffy hints that it is more than just a job: it is something which is very necessary: 'he sought approval without words to do what someone must'. If he does not record these events on film, the world may not know what has happened. His photographs have a deeper purpose – perhaps one which is worth the risks he takes to show 'how the blood stained into foreign dust'.

In the final stanza, the photographer reflects on how his work will be treated, aware that only a fragment of what he has produced will be used. The selection will be made by someone else, the editor, who 'will pick out five or six'. He is also particularly conscious of how people only dip into Sunday supplements, sensing that his power to move people or influence them will be short-lived. The photographer feels contempt for these superficial and temporary emotions, knowing that it is only in the brief space of time 'between the bath and pre-lunch beers' that his work can make any impact. Duffy uses 'prick with tears' to illustrate that the reaction barely affects the readers.

The last two lines show that he is disappointed at the indifference of the readers, for 'they do

Gas warfare

In the First World War, the Germans introduced many types of gas as weapons. These included tear gas, followed by the killing gases: chlorine, phosgene and mustard gas. The gases were fired from cylinders or shells. Mustard gas, which was introduced late in the war (July 1917) aimed to cause physical distress rather than death, although a small proportion of those affected did die. The fear of mustard gas was partly because it produced long-lasting effects, leading to such conditions as lung weakness and even blindness in many cases.

'The official medical history of the war gave:

Case four. Aged 39 years. Gassed 29 July 1917. Admitted to casualty clearing station the same day. Died about ten days later. Brownish pigmentation present over large surfaces of the body. A white ring of skin where the wrist watch was. Marked superficial burning of the face. The larynx congested. The whole of the trachea was covered by a yellow membrane. The bronchi contained abundant gas. The lungs fairly voluminous. The right lung showed extensive collapse at the base. Liver congested and fatty. Stomach showed numerous submucous haemorrhages. The brain substance was unduly wet and very congested.'

Different writers, different views

The extract from *Death's Men* opposite and above presents three sources written at the time of the war, and we can see the different ways in which the three writers quoted describe the effects of the gas attacks.

The writers are:
1 H. Allen, a soldier who wrote his memoirs of the war;
2 a nurse, Nurse Millard;
3 a doctor who wrote the official medical history.

Another soldier's account, quoted in Denis Winter's book, describes what it was like to prepare for a gas attack (see below).

… We gaze at one another like goggle-eyed, imbecile frogs. The mask makes you feel only half a man. You can't think. The air you breathe has been filtered of all save a few chemical substances. A man doesn't live on what passes through the filter – he merely exists. He gets the mentality of a wide-awake vegetable. You yourself were always miserable when you couldn't breathe through your nose. The clip on the gas mask prevents that…

How do the accounts of these writers differ? Think about:
- attitude
- language
- point of view
- style
- detail
- effect on the reader

Reading these extracts, you are perhaps able to gain a stronger impression of both the individual writers and the lives of the soldiers. The following are some of the questions you may wish to consider:

- How far do the different writers enable you to imagine what war is like for those involved?
- What have you discovered about the writers' own attitudes to the events they describe?
- What do the detailed descriptions of soldiers' physical conditions and symptoms make you feel about their lives?
- What do you learn about those who had to deal with the victims of war?
- Why do you think that the idea of gas attacks created such a sense of fear?

Testament of Youth

Background

Testament of Youth by Vera Brittain (1896–1970) is a most moving autobio-graphy of a young girl from a comfortable background who gave up her studies at Oxford University to enlist as a VAD nurse. Her brother and her fiancé were both killed in action in the First World War. She captures the pain of those who were involved in the fighting. Just as in the extract from Denis Winter's *Death's Men* (see pages 40-1), Vera Brittain gives a striking picture of those affected by gas warfare.

glossary

V.A.D. – Voluntary Aid Detachment

Convoys – lines of vehicles carrying troops

Glibly – easily, thoughtlessly

Orators – public speakers

Suppurating – oozing poison

Sic – The Latin word for 'thus', used by publishers to show that the spelling is the one intended, even if it is wrong: in this case, *temporally* should be *temporarily*

Testament of Youth

'NEVER IN MY LIFE have I been so absolutely filthy as I get on duty here.' I wrote to my mother on December 5th in answer to her request for a description of my work.

'Sister A. has six wards and there is no V.A.D. in the next-door one, only an orderly, so neither she nor he spend very much time in here. Consequently I am Sister, V.A.D. and orderly all in one (somebody said the other day that no one less than God Almighty could give a correct definition of the job of a V.A.D.!) and after, quite apart from the nursing, I have stoked up the stove all night, done two or three rounds of bed-pans and kept the kettles going and prepared feeds on exceedingly black Beatrice oil-stoves and refilled them from the steam kettles, literally wallowing in paraffin all the time, I feel as if I had been dragged through the gutter! Possibly acute surgical is the heaviest kind of work there is, but acute medical is, I think, more wearing than anything else on earth. You are kept on the go the whole time and in the end there seems nothing definite to show for it – except that one or two people are still alive who might otherwise have been dead.'

The rest of my letter referred to the effect, upon ourselves, of the new offensive at Cambrai.

'The hospital is very heavy now – as heavy as when I came; the fighting is continuing very long this year, and the convoys keep coming down, two or three a night… Sometimes in the middle of the night we have to turn people out of bed and make them sleep on the floor to make room for more seriously ill ones that have come down from the line. We have heaps of gassed cases at present who came in a day or two ago; there are ten in this ward alone. I wish those people who write so glibly about this being a holy War, and the orators who talk so much about going on no matter how long the War lasts and what it may mean, could see a case – to say nothing of ten cases – of mustard gas in its early stages – could see the poor things burnt and blistered all over with great mustard-coloured suppurating blisters, with blind eyes – sometimes temporally [sic], sometimes permanently – all sticky and stuck together, and always fighting for breath, with voices a mere whisper, saying that their throats are closing and they know they will choke. The only thing one can say is that such severe cases don't last long; either they die soon or else improve – usually the former; they certainly never reach England in the state we have them here, and yet people persist in saying that God made the War, when there are such inventions of the Devil about…

From the front lines
The letter to her mother gives a vivid account of the pressures of working in a hospital near the front lines.

- How clearly does Vera Brittain describe the tasks she has to complete?
- Make a list of all of them, showing the range of jobs she has to do.
- Why do you think she volunteered as a V.A.D. nurse?
- Considering she came from a prosperous family, what does this reveal about her character?

Qualities
From this list, pick out the relevant qualities which she shows:

Fear	Perseverance	Insensitivity	Courage
Adaptability	Humour	Laziness	Dedication
Self-pity	Anger	Selflessness	Commitment

God and the Devil
Study lines 26 to the end.

- What does this section show of Vera Brittain's attitude to people who talk about the war?
- What are her views on religion?
- How would your thoughts on war compare with Vera Brittain's?

The horror of gas

- How does Vera Brittain describe the gas cases? Compare her description with those of the nurse and the doctor in *Death's Men*. Which did you find more compelling?

Empathetic writing
Take some time to think about your feelings if you imagined yourself to be:

- Vera Brittain reflecting on a day's work;
- her mother on reading the letter;
- an injured soldier in the hospital ward where she was working.

Memories of the Battle of Britain

The County of Kent in the Second World War

Situated in the south-eastern corner of England, and separated from France by less than 30 kilometres at the shortest crossing-place (Dover to Calais), Kent saw more of the Second World War than any other part of the British Isles. Much of the Battle of Britain was fought in the skies over Kent. Such airfields as Biggin Hill were the bases from which the Spitfires and Hurricanes were launched.

In addition, the coastline was the departure-point for the armada of boats, large and small, which took part in the Dunkirk evacuation from the German forces advancing through France. (See also the comments on 'Night Patrol'.) Later, the coast was filled with ships preparing for the D-Day landings in Normandy in 1944, which started to drive the Germans back from their occupation of France.

Parts of Kent received evacuees, too, when the Government decided to send children away from cities and ports to the countryside, to protect them from the air-raids which made London and other cities particularly dangerous. The German bombers passed over Kent regularly on their way to London.

The Battle of Britain

The Dunkirk evacuation took place in June 1940, and the threat of a German invasion of Britain was strongest in the months immediately afterwards, since the Germans had pushed right through to the French coast. The Battle of Britain was fought in the months from July to October, and was won by the RAF despite the fact that the Germans had many more planes.

For the Germans, losing the Battle of Britain was a serious setback, since the idea of invading Britain had to be abandoned. For Britain, losing this battle would have been a complete disaster.

The passages in Tracks

Look at the passages 'The Schoolboy's Story' and 'Evacuees in Thanet', in the first section of the collection, called 'Front Lines'.

The Schoolboy's Story

The events which the writer, Mr Green, recalls come from June to October 1940. As he lived near Ashford, which is now on the direct route by Eurostar from London to France, the war came very close to him – much closer than for people living further north, for example. Very few people in, say, Yorkshire would have seen a live German airman or touched a German plane. The writer recalls vividly his life as a schoolboy in Kent at a time which he found very exciting.

The schoolboy's character
- From this passage, what do you discover about the schoolboy's character?
- Make a list of the features of his character and attitudes and find examples which support your points, such as the following:

characteristic	example
curious	cycling with a friend to see where a Messerschmitt had come down

Continue this list with your own choices and examples.

glossary

Pillboxes – small military buildings

MG – a type of sports car

Lord Haw-Haw – a Briton who worked for the Germans, giving out anti-British propaganda over the radio

Fuselage – main body of a plane

Magazine – container of ammunition

Swastika – the symbol of the Nazi party

The boy and the aeroplanes

The passage has a large number of references to aeroplanes, both British and German. Look closely at these, and think about the following questions:

- What do we learn about the different types of aeroplane the boy saw?
- What does he remember about the planes and the battles?
- How do the details he remembers show his fascination with the planes?

The style of the writing

Both this passage and 'Evacuees in Thanet' are taken from a collection of accounts by people who lived in Kent at the time of the Second World War and who are remembering their lives during the Battle of Britain.

- In what ways does the style of writing make you feel that these memories are those of someone who was a schoolboy at this time?
- How does the fact that the passage is written in the first person ('I' and 'we') help to bring the events alive?
- Looking back, how does the man feel about this period of his life?

Evacuees in Thanet

The area of Thanet is often called the Isle of Thanet, although it is not really an island. It contains the coastal towns of Margate, Broadstairs and Ramsgate, and still forms one of the main routes from England to France. This part of Kent was very exposed to the possibility of German attack, and during the evacuation from Dunkirk would have been full of people coming and going, with the Channel crowded with boats. This is one of Miss Coton's main memories.

When children became evacuees, they were often parted from their families, with very little idea of where they were going or what would happen to them. Frequently, they would be sent off with a suitcase or with a few clothes wrapped up in brown paper tied with string. They might have a label to say who they were and could be issued with a gas mask in case of attack. After the journey, they would be handed over to people they did not know, and might not see their parents for a long time.

glossary

Exodus – departure

Grisly – horrific

Miss Coton's memories

- How does Miss Coton suggest the confused feelings the children had about what was happening to them? Pick out some phrases from the passage which show this state of uncertainty.
- Why do you think she remembers so clearly what happened to the pets?
- The Home Guard, sometimes referred to as 'Dad's Army', consisted of volunteers who were protecting the country against possible invasion. What does the final incident in Miss Coton's story suggest about the Home Guard?
- How well does this passage capture the feelings of an evacuee?
- What impression of the war do you have from this passage? Pick out any words or phrases which you feel are important in giving this impression.

Writing Tasks

- 'I watched the little ships going to and from Dunkirk on beautiful bright clear days.' Write an eyewitness account to a friend in which you imagine this scene in detail.
- Study the picture of the young evacuee. Write her story.

Plymouth Hailed Victory At Midnight

While you are studying these pages, have your *Tracks* text open at the newspaper article 'Plymouth Hailed Victory At Midnight' by H P Twyford, Western Daily Herald, 15 August 1945.

The end of the Second World War

The end of World War II finally came with the surrender of the Japanese, brought on by the Allies' dropping of two atomic bombs on the cities of Hiroshima and Nagasaki. The war in Europe had ended three months earlier in May 1945, when Germany was defeated shortly after the suicide of Adolf Hitler. By this time, the war had gone on for six years, with many hardships and shortages of supplies for the people of Britain. Because of this, the sense of relief in the country was very great. Throughout the whole of Britain, celebrations and thanksgiving services marked the ending of the war.

Local celebrations

The Western Daily Herald gives a detailed account of how individuals and particular groups greeted the news in and around the city of Plymouth. At such a time of happiness and relief, the writer focuses on the many different ways in which the people of this particular region marked this event.

The city of Plymouth

A particular feature of Plymouth is its great importance, ever since the time of Sir Francis Drake and the Spanish Armada, as a naval base. Throughout the war, therefore, the city would have been, at least for a time, the home base of many British sailors, but also of servicemen and women from other Allied countries.

- Study carefully the references to people from the Armed Forces, noting which nationalities are mentioned.
- Why do you think that the article emphasises so strongly the celebrations of servicemen and women?

The layout of the article

Think about the use of:

○ the main headline ('Plymouth Hailed Victory At Midnight'):
- What are the key points to which this headline immediately draws the reader's attention?

○ the main sub-heading ('Heavy Downpour Failed to Damp Citizens' Jubilation'):
- What fresh information does this add?
- Why does the writer refer to the bad weather, and how does this reference emphasise the happiness of the people?

○ other sub-headings:
- How successful are these in encouraging the reader to continue to read the article?

- Compare the presentation and style with those of a modern newspaper. How differently do you think this story would be presented today?

Finding the right words

Any journalist describing an event such as this would be aiming to communicate a number of things, especially:

- o the importance of the day to the country;
- o the emotions of the people;
- o the drama of the scenes;
- o the details of the local celebrations.

The writer has clearly tried to use words which will seem grand and impressive, especially at the start of an article covering such historic moments.

- Think about the effect of quoting directly the Prime Minister's words.
- Study the following pairs of sentences and look at the differences between them. The first sentence of each pair is the one written by H P Twyford; the second states the same facts in simple, everyday language.
- Think about how successful the writer is in giving a greater sense of importance to his account by using such language.

The bonds of war snapped
The war ended

Most people were abed and asleep
Most people were sleeping in their beds

A nation was awakened from its slumbers
A country was awoken from its sleep

It spread on wings of lightning speed
The news travelled fast

- Find other sentences in the article where the writer has chosen language which underlines the sense of the importance or drama of the occasion, or has given a sense of the strong emotions of the people through colourful vocabulary.

The description of the celebrations

In the article, the writer describes a number of particular activities and celebrations.

- Find examples of references to:
  time
  movement
  sound
  emotions
  weather.

- Comment on how these contribute to the excitement of the celebrations.

Desperate Bosnians risk minefield deaths for US army rations

Maggie O'Kane In Mostar

NO ONE knew the dead woman's name. She lay in the basement corridor of Mostar hospital for a few hours, while a woman in a white bib and green overall mopped up her blood as it dripped slowly on to an icy tiled floor.

Her first name was Semsa. She was a refugee aged about 45. Saudin Guja met her in the crowd that flooded past his house at dawn to look for the emergency food aid air-dropped on the mountain by the Americans the night before.

He woke about 5a.m. as the crowd shuffled by his window, searching for packages they knew had been dropped in the night from the hum of the planes. He had heard nothing, but saw the crowd heading towards the field around Jeha Deiho's house on Ravinica hill.

He decided not to go, to stay in bed. The field was mined and only a few hundred yards from the front line with the Serbs. He was hungry but it was not worth the risk.

Blaguj has been cut off for months. The United Nations High Commissioner for Refugees has not visited, and the nine-mile road that leads to Mostar can be passed only at night. Sometimes a truck makes it through from Mostar with flour and oil, but it is not enough. Saudin had not eaten for two days.

For a while, he watched the crowd from his bedroom window coming back from Jeha Deiho's field carrying United States army rations.

Cardboard packages left over from the Gulf war, holding packets of chilli con carne and chicken à la king mix. Packages with Juicy Fruit chewing gum and brown plastic sachets of cherry and cocoa powder. Packages saying 'Made in Kansas City' in white letters.

Saudin kept telling himself the trip was too dangerous, but the returning crowd was euphoric and he was hungry. 'I saw old women coming down the street carrying bags full of the ration packs and then I couldn't stop myself,' he said.

He met Semsa just outside his front gate. He knew her as one of the refugees who had fled from the town of Stolac.

'Are the packages in Deiho's field?' she kept asking. 'It is for my children. I have nothing to cook for them. No food.'

They walked quickly. She talked about her children. He wondered if there would be anything left. On the way up, they were passed by two soldiers carrying an old man. His leg had been blown off by a mine in Deiho's field.

As they reached the field, they saw another explosion in the distance. A mine detonated by someone else scavenging for packages.

They kept going. Semsa kept talking about her children being hungry. He nodded, let her ramble on. As they reached the field, the Bosnian soldiers called to them: 'Don't go on, the field is mined.'

But nobody listened. 'They were calling to us: 'The Chetniks [Serbian soldiers] are at the end of the field, stay away.' But the people ran deeper and deeper into the minefield.

Another woman, a 22-year-old local called Colla, passed them on a stretcher. She had reached the hill at 5a.m. and picked her way carefully through the field. But looking up, she saw a woman about to step on a mine and called to her to watch out. Then one exploded under her feet, breaking the bones.

Semsa and Saudin had gathered about twelve packages when he heard shouts from the end of the field. 'Come on you Muslims. Come on over here and we'll give you some food.'

'The Chetniks were laughing at us,' Saudin said. Five Serb soldiers walked towards them. 'Come on Muslims, get your American parcels.'

They panicked. Semsa was running about five feet in front on him when she hit the mine. It blew her apart.

A second later, he felt the blast under his foot. He heard Semsa beside him. 'When she was dying, she kept repeating: "My children, my children."'

They buried her at night in Mostar graveyard, wrapped in a brown wool blanket, in a coffin made from a teak veneer wardrobe. On it, they wrote: 'Semsa'. No one knew anything else about the refugee from Stolac, who died on the mountain.

Maggie O'Kane, *The Guardian*, *27 November 1993*

glossary

Refugee – A person who has escaped from one place to seek safety in another

Air-dropped – Dropped by aeroplanes

Chilli con carne – A spicy minced meat dish

Sachet – small packet

Euphoric – overjoyed, extremely happy

Detonated – exploded, went off

Scavenging – trying to pick up things such as food, wherever they can be found

Veneer – A thin covering made of a high-quality wood

The article opposite, by Maggie O'Kane, comes from the *Guardian*, a **broadsheet** newspaper (*see* Glossary of Media Terms, p. 81), aimed at readers who like to read about topical issues of social concern. The articles are meant to make these readers think and they often feel strongly about what they are reading.

The headline

Study the headline:

- What do you notice about the style and form of this?
- How does it compare with other news headlines you have seen (think about broadsheets and tabloids)?
- What impact do the words of the headline have? (Do they make you want to read on? Why?)

The opening paragraph

Think about what opening paragraphs have to do:

- establish the themes;
- attract the reader's interest;
- set the emotional tone;
- convey a sense of immediacy.
- Note how **Maggie O'Kane** sets out to achieve these purposes. How successful is she?

The main text

This is a long article. Think about how it is constructed.

- Does the story divide into sections?
- Does it shift in its focus or keep a single centre of interest?
- What does the detail convey?

The ending

- In what ways does the final short paragraph add to the knowledge we have and our feelings about the event? Do you see any similarities between the first and last paragraphs?

Think about the following:

- Maggie O'Kane's style of writing;
- her ability to arouse sympathy;
- the focus on the story of Semsa;
- how Saudin helps her to develop the account;
- the way in which the desperate plight of the Bosnians is conveyed.

Inform, explain, describe: pointers for Question 3

The GCSE Syllabus sets out a number of ways of writing, which are assessed in different parts of the syllabus and examination.

- Question 3 on Papers 2F and 4H is designed to test candidates' ability to write according to the **range of writing:** inform, explain, describe.
- The topics set for this question ask writers to **use and adapt for specific purpose**.

The stimulus material from *Tracks* provides non-fiction content on which candidates may draw in their writing.

- Make sure that your writing covers properly what is required.
- You will find it helpful to think about the three words in turn, and look at the differences between them.

Inform

To **inform** means to tell someone something, to pass on **information**. Think about the qualities of a good informant who must be able to:

- present the information clearly;
- communicate facts accurately;
- help a reader to appreciate exactly what has happened.

Setting out your information well, whether in speaking or in writing, is one of the secrets of effective communication. It needs:

- a clear head;
- a logical mind;
- good organisation;
- effective use of language;
- a good grasp of facts – and figures, where appropriate.

Explain

To **explain** is to go a step further than simply informing. A good **explanation** is one which enables a listener or reader to understand, so when explaining it is necessary to:

- understand the topic fully – what the problem is, how something works, why something has happened;
- find ways of putting over the points so that any difficulties are sorted out, and any confusion cleared up;
- use a variety of means to deal with the need for technical explanations or clarifications.

A good explanation leaves the reader or listener clear, satisfied and free from doubt.

Describe

To **describe** is a kind of drawing in words. You may be asked to describe an object, a person, a scene or a series of events. A good **description** has the qualities of a good photograph or portrait. You can imagine that, if you have seen a crime being committed, the police will be very grateful for any **information**, and for an **explanation** of what has taken place. But a **description** of a place, an action or – especially – a person will be the most effective way of leading to an arrest. When describing, it is necessary to:

- use vivid, graphic words which will help someone to picture something or someone clearly;
- give as much relevant information as possible, as well as a general, overall description;
- be prepared to use images, including metaphors and similes;
- make sure that your reader or listener can follow clearly what you are saying;
- check that you have conveyed the fullest possible account.

Non-fiction specimen questions; questions 2 and 3 (2F/4H)

Question 2

Death's Men
- What features of a gas attack, as described in these extracts, made it feared more than many other forms of attack?
- In what ways do the three accounts of gas give different impressions because of their writers' different points of view?

Testament of Youth
- How do you feel that Vera Brittain's mother would have felt on receiving the letter describing Vera's work? Why?
- Does this extract suggest to you that Vera Brittain found her work as a V.A.D. rewarding? Explain your views.

Plymouth Hailed Victory At Midnight
- What light does this article shed on the attitudes of British people at the end of the Second World War?
- What does the article feel was special about the way in which the people of Plymouth marked the end of the war, and why?

The Schoolboy's Story
- In what ways does this story enable you to understand the life of a schoolboy in Kent at this time?

Evacuees in Thanet
- What impression does this passage give you about the difficulties facing a child who was about to be evacuated?

Desperate Bosnians
- In what ways does the article show that these people were indeed 'desperate Bosnians'?
- What do you find most disturbing in Maggie O'Kane's account of events?

Question 3

To help you to answer this question, you may use any of the selected material from 'Front Lines' in *Tracks*, but you may also draw on your own ideas.
- Write a report to a minister in the government of a war-torn country. Explain what the problems are in the centre of a war zone and set out clearly the needs of the people.
- 'Fear Of Famine Grows Daily'. Write an article, with this headline, for a newspaper in a country where food supplies are rapidly becoming scarcer because of war.
- 'How to deal with patients suffering from gas attacks.' Write a section for a manual, to be issued to all new nurses, on this subject. Include such topics as: preparing the nurses mentally for what faces them; understanding patients' feelings and symptoms; dealing with those seriously affected; practical, day-to-day routines.
- In a diary, give an account of 'a week at the front line', from the standpoint of either a soldier, a nurse, a journalist or a photographer.
- Imagine that you are taking part in a TV programme in order to explain to an interviewer the plight of people living in a war zone. The interview begins by asking the question: 'What is life like at present for the people of...?'
Write the script which follows.

Model answers: Question 2

- **In what ways does the article show that these people were indeed 'desperate Bosnians'?**

Maggie O'Kane is a journalist with an eye for close detail. She writes about the people in Bosnia in a clear, graphic style which brings home vividly to the reader the problems they face. The article is evidently meant to arouse a keen sense of sympathy for the plight of these people and an awareness of the horrors which war can inflict on civilians caught up in the fighting.

The word 'desperate' is a very appropriate one for her to use to describe these people. It shows a state of despair and a loss of hope. It can also suggest the actions of people who have become completely reckless, not worrying about their own safety; they will take any risks, no matter how serious. Desperate people can reach such a state that normal, everyday actions and behaviour seem simply futile. If they are to have any hope, they must resort to extreme measures in order to survive. They may lose their sense of caution and fail to calculate the dangers or the odds against success. Their physical or mental state drives them to ignore rational thoughts. If they are, as the Bosnians were, 'desperately hungry', they will go to any lengths to obtain food. This is the situation which Maggie O'Kane describes, and she does so in a way which enables the reader to concentrate on individual Bosnians, not the state of Bosnia itself.

It is easy for people in Britain, who are far away from the suffering, to become insensitive. O'Kane therefore deliberately focuses on one dead woman. This woman is said to be anonymous: 'no one knew the dead woman's name' are the first words of the article. The shocking description of her dead body, lying in a hospital corridor, emphasises her lack of identity. Yet she does have a first name, Semsa, as well as a story and personality. From the limited information available, Maggie O'Kane constructs as much as possible of her personal history: she tells us her age and her status ('a refugee aged about 45'), and we learn of her recent contacts with one other individual. We start to piece together the events which led to her death and we come to understand exactly why the adjective 'desperate' applies to her situation.

In the course of the unfolding of the story of Semsa, we discover many facts which remind us that she was certainly not the only one in such a situation. The story of the man who had met her, Saudin Guja, reveals that even those whose common sense warns them against going into the mined field to scavenge for the air-dropped food aid are so desperate that the sight of the food-carrying crowds overpowers the voice of reason. Even when they see mines detonating and Bosnians stepping on exploding mines they do not stop their search for packages.

Saudin and Semsa gave Maggie O'Kane the opportunity to 'put a human face' on the despairing Bosnians, whose towns and districts were cut off and whose food was limited to totally unsuitable packages dropped by American planes, with their contents of: 'Juicy fruit chewing gum and brown plastic sachets of cherry and cocoa powder'. O'Kane also enables us to understand clearly what drove Semsa to such extreme measures, as she was haunted by the thought of her starving children right up to the moment of her death. At the end of the passage, when the writer provides a close-up picture of Semsa's lonely makeshift burial, in a wardrobe converted into a coffin, no reader could doubt that they were 'desperate Bosnians'.

- **Does this extract suggest to you that Vera Brittain found her work as a V.A.D. rewarding? Explain your views.**

Because of the shortage of full-time nurses working close to the front lines, their numbers were supported by the Voluntary Aid Detachment (V.A.D.) nurses who volunteered to undertake nursing duties. We know that there were many young women like Vera Brittain who decided to become V.A.D. nurses because they felt that this would help them to contribute to the war effort. For those who had been brought up in comfortable, middle-class homes, as Vera had, the shock of the work must have been very great. In this passage, Vera does not hide the problems, and it must have been difficult for her mother to read in her letters about the kind of life her daughter was living, even though she had actually asked her for this description.

It seems from what Vera writes that her attitude towards her work was a complicated one. She definitely found it a completely new experience, as is clear from the start, where she writes that she has never before been 'so absolutely filthy'. The account of the working day shows how relentless the duties were, as she reports that she was: 'Sister, V.A.D. and orderly all in one'. The fact that there were insufficient staff is made very clear in this quotation, as she was doing three jobs in one. The strain of this must have been very great, but it was not the hard work as much as the terrible sight of the suffering and dying soldiers which was most difficult to bear.

It seems that Vera must have been very strong to survive the daily routine of duties. She was also very determined and courageous, since dealing with such endless streams of casualties must have made the nurses feel that they were fighting a losing battle: 'You are kept on the go the whole time and in the end there seems nothing definite to show for it'. They even had to move wounded soldiers out of their beds to make room for those who were still worse. This must have been physically exhausting as well as emotionally draining, since no doubt the soldiers who were being moved onto the floor were not very pleased about it and made their feelings known.

Vera was clearly very committed to what she was doing, but the sheer horror of the state of the victims of the gas attacks must have got her down. From what she writes, it would seem that she would have found the work much more rewarding if there had been something positive to show for it. However, because there were so many deaths there was hardly ever the sense of satisfaction which comes from saving lives and seeing people get better: 'One or two people are still alive who might otherwise have been dead'.

Perhaps Vera would have felt more rewarded if she had been able to maintain a strong belief in the rightness of the war. However, she had clearly become rather bitter and cynical about the kind of war propaganda ('those people who write so glibly about this being a holy War') which was put out during the First World War. She found it impossible to accept that the agony which these young soldiers suffered was justified. She believed that if the people who were very pro-war could only see the state of the gas victims — 'fighting for breath, with voices a mere whisper' — they would change their attitudes.

Throughout it all, Vera Brittain managed to keep her sense of humour. She even managed to joke to her mother about the difficulty of defining what the job of a V.A.D. was, when she wrote: 'No one less than God Almighty could give a correct definition'. She also showed a strong sympathy for the plight of the war victims and remained caring throughout. However, she found the experience demanding. Although she wished to do the best job she could, her sense of fulfilment in her work would have been far greater if the hours had not been so long and strenuous and the cases she saw so shocking. It was hard to continue to believe it was all worthwhile. Vera's thoughts about the futility and even wickedness of the war ('such inventions of the Devil') obviously affected her sense of the value of what she was doing.

Model answers: Question 3

- Imagine that you are taking part in a TV programme in order to explain to an interviewer the plight of people living in a war zone. The interview begins by asking the question: 'What is life like at present for the people of ... ?' Write the script which follows.

Interviewer: Good evening. This is John Abel reporting from war-torn Bosnia. I have here with me Shirley Greene, an aid worker who has agreed to be interviewed at the end of a sixteen-hour shift at a nearby refugee camp. Tell me. What is life like at present for the people of Bosnia?

Interviewee: The present situation for the Bosnians is unbelievably difficult. It is almost impossible to begin to imagine the suffering and hardship which the people are experiencing daily. Many of their towns are cut off from supply-routes and consequently food stores in shops have virtually disappeared. People were originally able to stock up with dry goods and other essentials, but these are now used up and almost all families have been reduced to the status of scavengers for whatever they can find on the streets or in the fields. As aid workers, we do what we can but there is so little we can achieve.

Interviewer: But surely the US planes are bringing much-needed food to the townspeople?

Interviewee: Oh, if only that were true! Unfortunately, the air drops are hardly helping at all. How useful is a package containing chewing-gum? The food is often unsuitable and simply unusable. For example, packets of dried food or drinks which require water are absolutely useless if there is none. Some food has been left over from past wars and is past its use-by date. And what is more, the packages are dropped in inaccessible or dangerous places. The Serb soldiers do everything they can to make things difficult. But even that is not the worst of it.

Interviewer: Do you mean to say there is more?

Interviewee: Yes. You see, land mines are the greatest problem. The whole area is strewn with the mines laid mainly by the Serbs, and this presents appalling difficulties for anyone travelling. Countless people have died or have been maimed. If you take the town of Mostar, for example, which is overrun with refugees from all over the district, the nearby fields are heavily mined and the town is surrounded by Serb soldiers. The recent food packages have tempted the distraught people of Mostar, and they have been streaming out of the town at the sight of the parcels dropping from the sky. Some have been lucky and have returned triumphantly clutching their rather pathetic offerings. But many have not. I have seen desperate women stooping to gather up the precious packs, putting their children's lives before their own. One unlucky foot on a mine, and they have lost limbs or even their lives.

Interviewer: Have you personally witnessed any particularly distressing cases?

Interviewee: Well, just today I have returned from the camp where the hard-pressed staff try valiantly to provide a proper medical service. One of the refugees had risked everything for the sake of her starving children, yet met her death tragically in a minefield. She was buried last night in a wardrobe, with no ceremony. She is just one more unknown victim. How many more must die in this way? It is not their fault. They are merely the victims in a war they cannot control. Much more aid is needed to help these unfortunate people.

Interviewer: Thank you, Shirley Greene, for your honest and revealing account. And, while distant bombing can be heard, this is John Abel returning you to the studio. Good night.

- **'How to deal with patients suffering from gas attacks.' Write a section for a manual, to be issued to all new nurses, on this subject. Include such topics as: preparing the nurses mentally for what faces them; understanding patients' feelings and symptoms; dealing with those seriously affected; practical, day-to-day routines.**

NURSES' MANUAL: SECTION 8 — GAS ATTACKS

Preparing for the worst

Nurses who are starting their duties in hospitals near the front line are advised that they will be faced with a new kind of casualty. This is as a result of the use by the enemy of poisonous gas as a weapon of war. You may well be faced with victims of different forms of gas, including chlorine. However, the most common gas you will find patients suffering from is mustard gas. It is especially important that you make yourselves thoroughly familiar with the symptoms and the stages which the patients may experience. You must be prepared for the worst. When the effects of gas become extreme, it is inevitable that the patient will die. At this stage all you can do is try to ease his suffering until the end comes.

Treating the patients

As with soldiers who are suffering from any disease or injury, a nurse's task is clear: to offer practical assistance and sympathy. Cleanliness and regular attention to patients' physical needs are vital. Words of comfort may well ease the pain and reduce distress or panic. Do everything you can to respond to the patients' requests, provided that these are in their best interests. Remember your duty as a nurse. Give patients all the support you can, but make sure that you do not let yourself become too involved. It is necessary to stay in control of your emotions and keep sufficient energy to respond to the demands of others in your charge. Some patients may ask for more than their fair share of your time. Do whatever you can, but be firm and fair at all times.

Medical symptoms

Study the effects of gas carefully, in order to make yourself fully informed:

(i)   Difficulty in breathing — Badly affected patients will find it difficult to breathe because of the effect of the gas burning the lining of the lungs.

Action:

Little can be done when this has occurred except basic nursing care.

(ii) First degree burns — These can affect the eyes, face or any other part of the body. They are agonising to endure.

Action:

Do not bandage or touch the burns.

Pour oil on the burns to relieve the pain.

Use propped-up sheets to form a tent.

Give a morphine injection in cases of extreme pain.

Overcrowding

New arrivals of seriously wounded or dangerously ill patients may well result in the need to redistribute the available beds. It is your responsibility to decide those who are in greatest need.

Action:

— Remove less severe cases from the beds and transfer them gently to the floor.

— Make sure that serious gas cases receive priority and urgent attention.

— Routines must be maintained, providing medicines and food and changing bedpans regularly.

ABOVE ALL, REMAIN CALM, FOCUSED AND COMPASSIONATE

Glossary of non-fiction terms

Argument – a series of points put together clearly to construct a clear case

Article – a piece of writing, on a particular topic, from a newspaper or magazine

Audience – the person or people being addressed by a speaker or writer

Autobiography – the story of someone's life (or part of that life), written by the actual person, sometimes with the help of a 'ghost-writer'

Biography – the story of someone's life (or part of that life), written by somebody else

Diary – a regular series of entries (e.g. daily) in a personal book which records one's experiences

Form – the kind and style of writing required for a particular purpose (e.g. article, letter, report)

Interview – a conversation (often on television or radio) between two people, with one (the interviewer) asking the questions of the other (the interviewee)

Journal – a more formal diary or record of daily proceedings, perhaps written for publication

Manual – a handbook, usually containing advice, information or instructions about an activity or product

Paragraph – a self-contained section of text, with a number of linked sentences contributing to a distinct set of ideas or information. The start of a paragraph is usually indicated, in a hand-written text, by beginning the first line slightly in from the left-hand margin

Report – an account of events, such as news items, or of an individual's or a group's ideas, delivered to an audience, e.g., a superior officer or the general public

Summary – a short version of a longer piece of writing (such as a book or article), giving only the main points.

media

Introduction

A range of media may be studied for this paper, as set down in the National Curriculum. Unseen materials for Papers 3 and 5 will be drawn from print-based media texts:

- advertisements
- brochures
- magazines
- leaflets
- newspapers
- mailshots.

You may be asked to work on one text or to compare one or more texts. Remember, you do not need to have followed a media studies course. The Glossary of media terms on page 81 will be helpful.

You should be able to take into consideration audience, purpose and style, both in commenting on texts and in producing your own texts in response to questions.

This section covers examples from some of the more common types of media source:

- newspaper articles
- advertisements
- leaflets
- mailshots

There are comments, points to consider and tasks for each source, as well as a further list of questions for you to work on (on page 74).

Newspaper sources

In your study of English, you will almost certainly have used newspapers on a number of occasions, perhaps for different purposes. You will have looked, perhaps, at the different types of newspapers, which are set out in the Glossary on page 81. There are many things to think about, for example:

- What is news?
- Are newspapers only about news?
- Can we believe what we read in them?
- Are they fair, or is there bias?
- How are stories presented?
- What part is played by photographs and other pictures?
- How do the layout and design of papers affect the reader?
- What are the main differences between tabloids and broadsheets?
- How do different sizes of print or use of different fonts influence the reader?
- What is the intended audience?

Newspapers can do a number of things:

- They can inform the reader.
- They can analyse events.
- They can try to persuade you.

These relate closely to the way in which you may be asked to respond to newspaper sources for Papers 3 and 5.

Responding to newspaper sources: an example

'Cyber pets will escape quarantine'
Carefully read the source set out opposite.

> *You should refer closely to the article when studying the topics below.*

The subject of 'quarantine' is one which has attracted a great deal of interest in recent years. It is a very controversial issue, and one on which many people feel strong emotions. There are several features of the way in which the article is written and set out which contribute to its effect. Think about the following features:
- headlines
- captions
- language
- use of individual cases and interviews
- illustrations
- graphics
- layout
- font size
- key words.

Are there other features which you think are important?

Using this list, consider carefully, by close reference to the article, the aims of the writer, and how the writer achieves these aims. How successful has the writer been? Discuss the extent to which the newspaper presents the issues about the subject fairly.
- Analyse the effectiveness of the presentation.
- Comment on the language and the argument.
- Look closely at the use of visual material.

You have now thought about the **content, design, purpose, effectiveness and language** of the article. There are other ways in which you may be able to think about this article and subject. For example, in the article, the writer invites further comment from readers, by:
- writing a letter;
- dictating a letter by phone.

Compose a letter to the newspaper in which you express your own opinions.

We are told that on, page 8 of the same newspaper, there is an **editorial** (see Glossary on page 81) on this subject. Look at the specimen question and the model answer on page 77.

> *Remember, on the Media paper, you will have one reading question (based on the content and how it is presented) and two writing questions, which use the text as a stimulus.*

Cyber pets will escape quarantine

Reunited

MICROCHIP TO ACT AS PASSPORT FOR ANIMALS

A REVOLUTIONARY microchip – no bigger than a grain of rice – is the key to ending the agony of quarantine for thousands of pet owners.

Under present anti-rabies regulations, dogs, cats and other pets have to be isolated in kennels for six months on arrival in Britain from abroad.

But under a new scheme to be unveiled by the Government this week, pets which have been vaccinated against rabies can be "tagged" with a special microchip and issued with their own "pet passport".

The chip is inserted in the pet's neck by syringe and checked with an electronic scanner similar to a supermarket checkout gun.

When an animal arrives in the country, it will be scanned. If the information on the chip matches the pet's papers, it can enter.

Distress

But animals being imported from countries where rabies is rife will still have to endure the solitary confinement.

News of the change – which is expected to become law next year – has been welcomed by pet owners.

Apart from the distress caused to their pets, they have campaigned against quarantine for three reasons:

COST: To keep their family pets in quarantine for six months, owners have to pay £1,387 for a dog and £1,279 for a cat.

The RSPCA estimate that the new system – which would involve buying an import licence, vaccination, blood testing and the microchip implant – would cost between £300 and £400 – a massive saving.

Sun SPECIAL REPORT

DEATHS: Three thousand animals have died in quaranting since 1975.

SMUGGLING: Customs officers are constantly catching people trying to bring pets into Britain illegally.

RSPCA official Alex Ross said: "We have been campaigning for this for some years. We believe vaccinating animals against disease is safer and just as effective as quarantine. And it is more humane."

Lady Mary Fretwell, who runs the campaign group Passports for Pets, said: "We very much welcome that the Government has finally grasped the nettle on this and hope there are no more delays. I have betrayed my dogs three times in 30 years by putting them in quarantine.

June Hamilton, of the Quarantine Abolition Fighting Fund, said: "I am delighted that at last we are getting some action. It was recommended to the Government in 1994 that the system should be scrapped. Since then we would estimate 80 to 100 animals have been smuggled into Britain every week."

Pressure

The scale of the problem is revealed by figures which show that last year 4,028 dogs, 3,351 cats, 692 chinchillas and 434 rabbits were among animals quarantined.

Among those who have suffered are the Fraser family of Kew, Surrey.

They visit their 18-month old cat Amy every Saturday afternoon in kennels at Willowslea Farm in Stanwell Moor, Surrey. Amy returned with the family two months ago from Vietnam where husband Paul worked in the construction industry for two years.

He and his wife Alicia and two daughters Roya, 11 and Taya, 8, are faced with making the trip every week for the next four months.

Alicia, 43, said: "It is terrible. The only day we can visit is Saturday because the children are in school. Amy is always very pleased to see us. She rubs herself against our legs and purrs. Six months is such a long time."

The Government decided last October to review the current quarantine arrangements after coming under mounting pressure from animal welfare groups and pet owners.

WHAT DO YOU THINK?

What do you think about the plan to scrap the quarantining of pets? Write to: PETS, The Sun, 1 Virginia St, London E1 9BW.

Advertisement sources

Advertising

Advertising is the use of techniques to sell products or services, by appealing to a reader, viewer or audience.

- ○ People advertise through the use of different **media**, which include:

television	newspapers
cinema	magazines
radio	publicity leaflets
posters	mailshots.

- ○ Advertising may seek to:

persuade	flatter
tempt	appeal to vanity or greed
excite	raise aspirations or expectations.

- ○ Advertisements tend to:
  select information to suit a purpose;
  aim at a particular audience (targeting) by sex or age, or a particular social group or interest group.

- ○ Advertisements rely heavily on:
  hard-hitting slogans or catchphrases
  jingles (tunes with words)
  unusual visual images
  unexpected ideas or new twists.

Charity advertising

In this section you can see examples of **charity advertisements**. These are a type of source-material frequently used as a stimulus in examination papers (Papers 3 and 5). Other types of advertising are shown in the sections on **leaflets** (page 64) and **mailshots** (page 68).

The two advertisements here were issued by 'Oxfam' and 'Help the Aged'.

Both are major charities which are well-known and have operated for a long time.

Both are asking for a response to the situations of people in developing countries.

One is a direct money-making appeal. The other is a competition, designed to raise awareness of social issues.

SHE HAS NOWHERE LEFT TO TURN.

PLEASE DON'T TURN THE PAGE

You could be Tsering's last hope. She has little or no food to eat, and lives in a tiny, insanitary mud shack. Without help soon she could die.

Yet by sponsoring an elderly person like Tsering for just £10 a month, you could provide the food, clothing and medicines they need to survive.

In return, you'll receive regular reports on your adopted grandparent. For more details, please complete the form below.

Yes, I'm interested in helping an elderly person overseas. Please send me details.

Mr / Mrs / Miss / Ms _____

Address _____

_____

Postcode _____ Tel. No. _____

Return to:
Helen Higgs,
Adopt a Granny
Help the Aged
FREEPOST
London
EC1B 1JY

Help the Aged

Adopt a Granny
Registered Charity No. 272786

We're looking for winning designs for a brand new range of mugs

- Your design can be any colour or shape as long as it looks good on a standard sized mug.
- Your slogan could be a word, a phrase, or a whole sentence as long as it sums up what *Fair Trade* means to you.

The prize

The winning design will be put on to mugs by workers in a *Fair Trade* ceramics factory in Thailand, and sold in Oxfam *Fair Trade* shops.

Each winner will receive

- a set of six mugs, presented in their local Oxfam shop
- £100 worth of development-education resources for their school.

The press will be there to see you collect your prize.

This is *Fair Trade*

All too often, the farmers who grow much of the food we buy in our supermarkets are paid barely enough to live on. Take bananas, for instance.

Felix Bernard, a banana farmer in the Windward Islands, is having a tough time. The price he gets for his crop at market has fallen drastically in the last few years. He and other farmers can't compete with powerful transnational companies which have driven many of the world's smaller producers out of business.

Farmers like Felix depend on bananas. They need a fair price for their crop, or they'll go out of business. A *Fair Trade* banana could be one way to secure the future prosperity of the islands. Oxfam is working with farmers to help them to produce high-quality bananas for the *Fair Trade* market.

Look our for these bananas in your supermarket. Buy them and you'll be *Fair Trading*.

How to enter

You can enter the competition in one of two age categories: 14-16 years or 16-18 years (sixth form). The winning designs will be used on mugs to be sold in Oxfam's *Fair Trade* shops.

Feel free to use any medium - paint, gouache, crayon, pastel, ink, or any other. Be innovative. You want your design to be head and shoulders above the rest.

Write your name, address, school and age clearly on the back of your entry and send it to: Liz Leaver, Oxfam Campaigns, 274 Banbury Road, Oxford OX2 7DZ.

Closing date: 30 November 1998

fast with Oxfam on 13 November 1998
Find out more. Call the fastline on 0990 084225   **Oxfam's fast**

Oxfam GB is a member of Oxfam International. Registered Charity No. 202918.   Code:103039   SC/152H/98

you'd be a mug to miss out

enter our exciting competition

Oxfam's fast
13 November 1998
SEE OVER FOR DETAILS ▶

Looking at advertisements

Although the examination will use printed advertisements, the use of different forms of advertising in preparation and coursework will certainly be helpful, to think more fully about advertisers' techniques.

People are generally most aware of television or radio advertisements. By thinking about these, you can identify the different ways in which advertisers try to work on people to make them buy a product. In the past, advertising often contained a 'hard sell', in which the listeners or viewers had the message about the product 'rammed down their throats'. Nowadays, advertisers more often go for subtler approaches, often so subtle that it is difficult to be sure what is being advertised or why a particular image or storyline is used.

- **Analyse advertisements you know, from various sources, thinking about the selling techniques employed.**

Some questions to discuss
- How much are you influenced by advertisements?
- Which *medium* of advertising (e.g. radio, magazines) do you find most effective, and why?
- Choose two advertisements, one which you find particularly effective and one which you do not. Analyse why. (Compare your choices with a friend, and discuss.)
- How do advertisers target the young? Does this have any desirable or undesirable effects?
- Advertisers are sometimes referred to as 'hidden persuaders'. Does this seem to you an appropriate term or not?

Comparing advertisements
Many examination questions ask for a comparison of two advertisements. If you compare the Oxfam and Help the Aged advertisements, you could look at, for example:

- immediate impact
- visual techniques
- use of captions or slogans
- content of text
- tone of language
- target audience
- action required.

> **Question 1** *concentrates on content, language, layout and design.*
> **Question 2** *may ask you to adapt the content or form for a particular writing purpose: analyse, comment, review.*

Leaflet sources

Publicity leaflets

Publicity leaflets may be issued for a variety of purposes. They may be a direct or indirect form of advertisement, but their common aim is to provide information about an organisation. To examine the effect of different forms of leaflet:

○ Make a collection of leaflets which you have obtained from a variety of sources. These may come from such places as: stations, libraries, tourist information offices, hotels.

○ See what different types you can collect, what range of services or products are covered, and what information they contain.

Leeds Castle

- Study the Leeds Castle leaflet carefully, noting down the information you learn from it, the selling-points which are stressed, and the way in which the pictures and text are used together.
- Look at the specimen questions on page 74 and the model answer on page 78.
- If you were going to answer the question about a new facility for Leeds Castle, what would your suggestion be?
- Choose one other castle or famous building known to you, and prepare a publicity leaflet to advertise it.
- If you have time, practise one or both of the specimen questions, giving yourself no more than 35–40 minutes, as in a GCSE examination.

A castle for all seasons.

EEDS Castle, one of the most romantic and most ancient castles in the Kingdom. In the 9th century, this was the site of a manor of the Saxon royal family. Listed in the Domesday Book, this castle has been a Norman stronghold, a royal residence to six of England's mediaeval Queens, a playground and palace to Henry VIII and a private home.

Today, lovingly restored and now administered by the Leeds Castle Foundation, it is home to a magnificent collection of mediaeval furnishings, paintings, tapestries and treasures. This is a place where visitors of the present meet with lives of

the past. You sense it, walking the grounds, where even the leaves breathe history.

HISTORIC PARK AND GARDENS.

The crowning glory of this most English of castles is its setting. On two small islands in the midst of an encircling lake, surrounded by a green arc of parkland, thick with trees and hills that tumble gently down to the water's edge. Within the 500 acre park, there are woodland walks, lakes and waterfalls, gardens and greenhouses. And so many glorious castle views, Kings and Queens and seasons may change, but Leeds Castle's enchanting and very English beauty is lasting, whatever the time of year.

ROYALTY AND ROMANCE.

The castle was first built in stone by

Norman barons nearly 900 years ago to overawe the English. On Edward I's accession, it was conveyed to the Crown, and for the next three centuries was a royal palace; fortified, enlarged, enriched and much loved by successive English Kings and Queens.

Love, romance and happiness have been in the air at Leeds Castle down the centuries; certainly for Queen Eleanor of Castile, Catherine de Valois and Henry VIII, the most celebrated of all the owners.

THE LEEDS CASTLE FOUNDATION FUNDING THE FUTURE.

A past that's not preserved, soon becomes a past that is forgotten. Leeds Castle was saved for the nation when Lady Baillie, the last private owner, established the Leeds Castle Foundation on her death in 1974. The objectives of this independent charitable trust are to preserve the castle and park in perpetuity for the benefit and enjoyment of the public; to enable use of the castle for important national and international meetings, particularly for the advancement of medical research and for the furtherance of peace; and to promote artistic and cultural events.

Leeds Castle receives no major grants or government funding. The income raised from visitors, conferences, private functions and special events (including open-air concerts), is essential for the continued conservation of this important heritage site for future generations.

LEEDS CASTLE

Maidstone in Kent

ADY Baillie's purpose and ambition was to preserve Leeds not merely as history, but as 'a living castle'. Now adults and children of all ages, nationalities and interests, enjoy the great variety of things to see and do in the castle and park. Living testimony that the ambition is realised. To make the most of it all, allow around 3 to 4 hours for your visit.

THE CASTLE DEFENCES.

The Barbican, Fortified Mill and Gatehouse form part of the castle's concentric defence system, developed by Edward I in the 13th

century. Revetment towers, arrow slits and murder holes are a reminder of Leeds original function – an impregnable fortress.

THE CASTLE AND TREASURES.

Richly furnished and decorated throughout with carved beams, Tudor stonework, fine wallhangings and Flemish tapestries – each room is teeming with treasures. You'll walk through history. From the Norman cellar to the mediaeval Gloriette, from Henry VIII's Banqueting Hall and the royal chapel, to the beautiful drawing rooms created in the 1930s. Their stories and secrets are brought alive for you by the castle guides in each room.

CULPEPER GARDEN.

Created in 1980 and named after the Culpeper family, 17th century owners of Leeds Castle. Like a cottage garden on a grand scale, it's a perfect setting for a delightfully informal collection of English flowers – roses, pinks, lad's love, lavender and lupins – many with wonderful scents. A herb border heightens the fragrance.

THE AVIARY.

This spectacular modern aviary was opened by H.R.H. Princess Alexandra, Royal Patron of the Leeds Castle Foundation, in 1988. It houses a collection of more than 100 rare species of bird, and aims not only at conservation, but also at successful breeding – to reintroduce endangered species into their original habitats.

WOOD GARDEN AND PAVILION GARDEN.

Conceived in the 1920s as a 'green garden', it is especially lovely in spring with its carpets of daffodils, narcissi and wood anemones bordering the meandering streams and small lakes. Later, azaleas and rhododendrons emblazon these gardens.

THE DUCKERY.

Created in the 1960s out of a wilderness of tangled brambles and fallen trees, it is now the natural habitat for a fine collection of unusual and exotic waterfowl – pintail, mandarin and eider ducks, red-breasted Russian geese, black swans, even peacocks – which also roam free within the grounds.

DOG COLLAR MUSEUM.

Hunting dogs, gundogs, mastiffs to guard the castle gate, spaniels and lapdogs to grace the apartments of widowed Queens. Down the years, dogs have been part of life at Leeds Castle. So it is appropriate that here is the world's finest collection of antique dog collars, with examples ranging over 400 years.

FAIRFAX HALL AND TERRACE ROOM RESTAURANTS.

Snacks, salads, cream teas and a good variety of hot meals are available with a choice of

fast food in the Stable Yard, self-service meals in the 17th century Fairfax Hall or a table service menu in the Terrace Room. Lovely gifts and souvenirs are available from shops, both nearby and at the park entrance – where there is also a parkland picnic site.

Children love getting lost in the maze and it's fun for grown-ups too. At the centre a

viewing mound – a hollow dome – a grotto that takes you from the light of day into a fantastic underworld of beasts and legends, tunnels and tumbling water.

1998 SPECIAL EVENTS AND ENTERTAINMENTS.

✤ New Year's Day Treasure Trail – 1 Jan.

✤ A Celebration of Easter – 11 to 13 April.

✤ Festival of English Food & Wine – 16 & 17 May.

✤ Balloon & Vintage Car Fiesta – 6 & 7 June.

✤ Annual Open Air Concerts, Royal Liverpool Philharmonic Orchestra with the Band and Guns of the Royal Artillery – 27 Jun & 4 Jul (advance tickets only).

✤ Flower festival – 16 to 19 Sept.

✤ Grand Firework Spectacular – 7 Nov.

✤ Christmas Celebrations – decorations, floodlighting and carollers from mid-Dec. Christmas Shop from 1 Nov.

✤ Half-term Fun for Children activities during Kent school holidays.

✤ Kentish Evening Dinners many Saturdays throughout the year. (inc. tour of castle, five course meal, wine and entertainment) 7pm to 12.30am (by reservation).

OPEN EVERY DAY (Except Christmas Day).

March to October Park & Gardens 10am to 5pm★. Castle 11am to 5.30pm★. (Ticket office closes 5pm.) November to February Park & Gardens 10am to 3pm★. Castle 10.15am to 3.30pm★. (Ticket office closes 3pm.)

★ **Last admission. Park & Gardens close two hours after last admission.**

(Closed 27th June, 4th July prior to Open Air Concerts.)

♿ Disabled visitors are especially welcome. Full details of accessibility and special facilities throughout the castle and grounds are given in a special leaflet available on request in advance, or on arrival.

We regret no dogs except guide dogs and hearing dogs.

The trustees reserve the right to close all or part of the castle as necessary.

TOURS FROM LONDON.

Britainshrinkers – 01963 34616. Evan Evans Tours – 0181 332 2222. Frames Rickards – 0171 837 3111. Golden Tours – 0171 233 7030. Green Line – 01634 832666. Travellers Check-In – 0171 636 7175. Venice Simplon-Orient-Express – 0171 805 5100. For further details and bookings contact the company direct, your hotel porter or concierge, or a tourist information centre.

For information and news 24 hours a day, call – Leeds Castleline 0891 800680.★★

Leeds Castle, Maidstone, Kent ME17 1PL

Tel: (01622) 765400. Fax: (01622) 735616

Internet http://www.se-eng-tourist-board.org.uk/seetb//(see places to visit).

For information 24 hours a day, call our Special Events Line on 0891 800656★★

★★ Calls cost 39p per minute cheap rate and 49p per minute at all other times.

The best day out in history.

Mailshot sources and promotional literature

Sending mailshots

'Accident Protection Plan' is one of many companies which send out promotional envelopes to a large number of houses. These are often termed 'junk mail' – by those who receive them rather than those who send them.

The example below is from a recent mailing of a large pack of leaflets and letters in a thickly-packed envelope. Those who send out such mailshots are usually trying, directly or indirectly, to sell a product or service. If they were not, there would be no point in their doing it.

Many people who receive what they regard as 'junk mail' automatically throw it out without looking at it.

- **Think about** how APP tries to stop you wanting to throw away their mailshot.
- **Consider**:
  layout
  language
  tone
  selling-points
- **Decide**:
  at whom it is aimed;
  whether you think it is effective;
  how it might be improved.

APP

Accident Protection Plan

APP House, 120-125 Dickens Mews, London WCC1 44XX

Mr A Brown
2 Fairmile Road
Paxton
London
W4 5SD

Tuesday 29th September 1998

Dear Mr Brown,

<u>We are delighted to tell you that you have won a prize</u> with Lucky Number 2845815 in our **NEW £200,000 CASH DRAW.**

What have you won? It may be the **£25,000 TOP CASH AWARD**. Or maybe one of **FIVE £1,000** or **TWENTY £300 Cash Wins,** or one of 1,000 special Accident Protection Plan rollerball pens.

To claim your <u>confirmed win</u>, simply **FILL IN THE SPECIAL FORM enclosed and post it** in the reply-paid envelope to reach us by the closing date 31st October 1998. If you have won the top award of £25,000 you can double your money if you send the form back within seven days.

A Commissioner for Oaths has already drawn the winning numbers at random – and YOURS is one of them!

Before you fill in the form, we would like you to consider this offer of accident insurance. Imagine what would happen to a relative or friend, who suffered an injury and could never lead a normal life again. **Everyone is at risk,** driving, on the train or the bus, in an aeroplane, or even just crossing the road!

Suppose a victim of a sporting accident survived – but lost the use of his or her legs. Wouldn't receiving a **CASH Lump Sum of £75,000** help them to come to terms with their disablement? The Accident Disablement Protection Plan costs <u>less than 10 pence</u> a day and gives you protection world wide. You can also have **extra cover** for special risks.

DON'T DELAY!! Take out an Accident Protection Plan Policy today. Don't forget, **all you have to do is fill out the back of the form claiming your prize.** We will do the rest.

Barclays Insurance leaflet

From the leaflet on this page and page 70, you can see that Barclays Bank is also trying to sell insurance. There is a single sheet, double-sided.

Notice the particular selling-points used: if Barclays wishes you to change from your existing company, you must be persuaded. The message is therefore a direct one. It stresses:

- ○ value
- ○ opportunity
- ○ service
- ○ additional features.

- Pick out the examples of how Barclays tries to tempt the reader. What would be most likely to encourage you to change to Barclays? Why might you decide not to?
- To whom is this leaflet trying to appeal? Is it successful?
- Compare the two approaches of the insurance companies. Which of these is more likely to attract you and to make you want to buy? Why?

Quality cover, guaranteed lower premiums. An offer that's too good to miss.

As a Barclays customer, not only can you now enjoy the benefits of quality car insurance, but we even guarantee to beat your current renewal premium. Our flexible car insurance can be arranged over the phone with the minimum of fuss and no lengthy form to fill out. As well as taking the hassle out of purchasing car insurance, our unique offer, combined with quality cover, guarantees you a great deal.

As well as excellent cover, you can expect far more for your money

From the moment you choose Barclays Car Insurance, you can expect a service which not only gives real value for money, but also offers a range of benefits you'll find hard to beat. What's more, you'll begin to enjoy the extra peace of mind which comes from knowing you

have dedicated professionals working on your behalf. After all, Barclays are one of the world's leading and most respected financial organisations.

With our tailor-made cover, we'll treat you as an individual

Your unique documentation is tailored to you, clearly explaining only the cover that you've asked for and making your policy simple and easy to understand.

Our comprehensive car insurance policy offers the following features:

1. We authorise all repairs fast

In the event of your vehicle requiring repair work, the last thing you'll want is any unnecessary delay. That's why, at Barclays, we use the latest video technology to authorise repairs swiftly and efficiently. And you'll have access to our 24 hour accident recovery line, 365 days of the year. Add to this the fact that our repair network incorporates only the very best repair specialists, and you can rely on expert assistance,

when you need it most. And all repairs are fully guaranteed for 3 years.

2. A courtesy car, absolutely free

Should you need to make a claim, we'll do everything we can to make things easier for you. For instance, we'll provide a courtesy car totally free of charge for the duration of the repairs (providing your vehicle is being repaired by a Barclays approved repairer). And that's not all, your repaired car will be cleaned inside and out before it's returned to you.

3. Replacement cover for all audio equipment

Subject to a reasonable excess, our unlimited audio equipment cover means that in the event of theft or damage, you have the peace of mind

of having everything fully covered, and that we can normally replace the equipment within a few days.

Please note that in order to take advantage of our guarantee you will need to:

1. Pay your premium in one payment by Connect Card, Barclaycard or by most other debit or credit cards.

2. Provide proof of your renewal premium.

To save time when you call, please remember to have your renewal documents to hand.

N.B. This guarantee cannot apply to renewal premiums issued by Barclays Car Insurance.

Offer expires 30th July 1999

We are not able to provide quotes for:

• Motorcycles
• Commercial vehicles
• Cars used for business only

Call now on 0870 600 1414 quoting ref 9813 or fill in the coupon

And remember, if you require cover to commence within the next 30 days, please telephone us immediately on the number provided. Lines open 8am-9pm weekdays, 9am-Saturday 5pm.

Analyse, review, comment: pointers for Question 2

As was mentioned on page 50, the GCSE syllabus sets out a number of ways of writing which are assessed in different parts of the syllabus and examination.

- Question 2 on papers 3 and 5 is designed to test candidates' ability to write according to the **Range of Writing: Analyse, Review, Comment**.
- The main assessment objective is **to adapt writing for particular purposes and audiences.**
- The supporting assessment objectives are to:

  organise ideas into sentences and paragraphs;
  use grammatical structures of Standard English;
  use a wide vocabulary;
  express meanings with clarity and precision.

You will need to read the question carefully to see how it relates to one or more of the three words 'analyse', 'review' and 'comment'. The question will be based closely on the media text or texts provided for the examination, which will have been studied for Question 1. (In question 1 candidates write on the content of the texts, being assessed for reading.) For question 2, candidates will be assessed on their ability to **write in a particular way**, related to the range of writing mentioned above: the form might be a letter, or report, for example.

Analyse

Analysis is a term used in different subjects of the curriculum. In English, analysis usually consists of the close examination of texts, studying, for example:

- their form;
- their language;
- their structure;
- their purposes.

Analysis is often the first part of a process: after breaking something down into its parts, we usually need to put it together again, now that we can see how it works: this is the process of synthesis.

- **Ask yourself questions about the different ways of analysing text:**
  Form   – the kind of text; the design of the text;
  Language – straightforward? ornate? factual? ironic? direct? subtle?
  Structure – simple or complex?
  Purposes – inform, explain or describe?
              – analyse, review, comment?
              – argue, persuade, instruct?

Review

To review something is, at its simplest, to 'look at it again'. The most common kind of review with which you are likely to be familiar in English is the book review, where you may be asked to:

- give your response;
- explain your reasons;
- offer an opinion;
- make a recommendation.

71

For Question 2, you may be asked, as part of your response, to:
- review the evidence and decide what it tells you;
- review different approaches and judge their suitability or effectiveness;
- review advantages and disadvantages and come to a conclusion or recommend a solution.

You should be aware that the process of **review** will also require close **analysis** and involve making **comment**.

Comment

We comment on people or objects for various reasons and in different ways, but mainly to express our opinion of them. The same is true when commenting on texts or arguments. It is important to think about the reasons why we comment and the kinds of comment we make. These may be to express:
- approval
- amusement
- delight
- praise
- admiration
- disgust
- relief.

In an English response, much more is needed. You may need to comment on:
- **what** your reactions or views are;
- **why** you feel or think as you do;
- **how** you think someone should act.

Comment, therefore, must be **clear** and **personal**, but also **well-argued** and **fully-supported**.

NB Whether the writing is **analysing**, **reviewing** or **commenting**, or all three, it is important for it to be in the appropriate style.

> *Remember the main assessment objective!*

Argue, persuade, instruct: pointers for Question 3

- Question 3 on papers 3 and 5 is designed to test candidates' ability to write according to the **range of writing : argue, persuade, instruct.**
- The main assessment objective is **to adapt writing for particular purposes and audiences.**
- The supporting assessment objectives are to:
  organise ideas into sentences and paragraphs
  use grammatical structures of Standard English
  use a wide vocabulary
  express meanings with clarity and precision.

You will need to read the question carefully to see how it relates to one or more of the three words, 'argue', 'persuade' and 'instruct'.
- **Argue:** You will be expected to develop a case or point of view; sometimes the question will ask you to present *both sides* of an argument and weigh up the strengths and weaknesses of each, coming to a conclusion.

○ **Persuade:** You will need to *convince* a reader or audience of what you are saying: you may wish to persuade someone of your view, or to change their mind, or to join a political party or campaign.
○ **Instruct:** Your task will be to *teach* someone how to do something, or give them *orders* or *instructions* on what to do.

For this question, candidates may be asked to consider points from the stimulus material used in question 1 or to choose their own context for writing of this kind.

Argue

An argument should be clear, well-constructed and logical. The steps should follow as in a mathematical proof.

The word *therefore* (so, thus, hence, consequently) concludes an argument. Other connecting words help to develop it, such as:
○ and/but/for
○ moreover/however/because
○ also/nevertheless/since

Arguments should be: factual, objective, clear and unemotional

Persuade

How do you persuade someone?
○ Be confident;
○ Be convinced;
○ Be convincing;
○ Be conclusive;

○ Use a range of effective techniques;
○ Think of what persuades *you*;
○ Think of skilled persuaders.

A good persuader uses **rhetorical devices** (the tricks of public speakers) such as:
○ rhetorical questions;
○ exclamations;

○ direct appeals to the reader or listener;
○ colourful images and soundbites.

Instruct

This section is set out as a simple set of instructions:
You must speak or write in such a way that:
○ someone can follow a set of procedures;
○ you pass on your skills by clear explanations;
○ you make sure that what needs to be done is done;
○ the audience learns or understands the new knowledge required.

You should:
○ take things step by step, in a clear, simple structure;
○ give commands ('Do this...') or prohibitions ('Avoid this...') which are firm and direct;
○ check understanding at key stages.

Do not:
○ make things too complicated;
○ lose the thread;
○ write long sentences.

Non-fiction specimen questions: Questions 1, 2 and 3

The questions for Question 1 and Question 2 are to be answered with reference to media sources such as those earlier in the chapter. Some of the questions refer directly to the sources given on these pages, but you may choose other examples of your own choice on which to base your response. Question 2 on Papers 3 & 5 is designed to test candidates' ability to write according to the range of writing: analyse, review, comment.

Questions 1 & 2

Newspapers

Q 1   Study two articles, one from a broadsheet and one from a tabloid (or from different tabloids), which are written on the same subject. Summarise clearly the information and feelings conveyed by each, and show how the layout, presentation and language of each of these contribute to their effect.

Q 2   Write a newspaper 'leader' or editorial based on the issues raised in one of the articles.

Advertisements

Q 1   What are the ways in which each of these advertisements seeks to appeal to the reader? (Consider all relevant considerations of language, content and design.) Comment on the target audience at which you think that the advertisers are aiming.

Q 2   Write the report which you will present at your School Council, which puts forward three methods by which you intend to advertise the chosen school charity. Think about audience, style and use of media.

Leaflets

Q 1   Study carefully the attached publicity leaflet (pages 65–7). What does this tell you about the attractions of Leeds Castle and its suitability for a family day out? How clear do you find the layout and why?

Q 2   Write a letter to the managing director of the Leeds Castle foundation in which you set out your ideas for developing the site. You should analyse the possibilities offered by the buildings and grounds and comment on the advantages which your proposal will bring.

Mailshots and promotional literature

Q 1   You have obtained two types of promotional literature on the subject of insurance (see pages 68–70). Compare the effectiveness of the two approaches to promotion in making you want (a) to read them, and (b) to take the desired action.

Q 2   Imagine that you are an advertising executive, working for a mailshot company which is about to launch a new campaign. Put forward your proposals for a mailshot which will persuade people to take out insurance.

Question 3

Question 3 on papers 3 and 5 is designed to test candidates' ability to write according to the range of writing: Argue, Persuade, Instruct.

Q 1   Write a letter to the leader of your local Council, Ms Brown. In this, you should try to persuade the council not to grant permission for the building of another out-of-town supermarket which you believe will ruin the shops in the High Street.

Q 2   For a school Open Day, you have been asked to organise eight Year 11 (sixteen year-old) pupils to escort a group of prospective parents on a tour of the school. Write a sheet of clear instructions which will enable them to perform this task well.

Model answers: Question 1

- **What are the ways in which each of these advertisements seeks to appeal to the reader? (Consider all relevant considerations of language, content and design.) Comment on the target audience at which you think that the advertisers are aiming.**

These two advertisements feature two of Britain's best-known charities. 'Help the *Aged*' and 'Oxfam' are known for their campaigns of trying to bring aid to those in desperate need, and their names are familiar to large numbers of people.

These charities often appeal for financial help, and probably on seeing the name 'Oxfam' many people will immediately think that this is just another appeal for money. But when you look at the advertisement closely, it is clear that this is a different kind of appeal. It is, in fact, more of an invitation, or challenge. No money is asked for, and there is not even an entry fee for the competition which is advertised. If you are successful in the competition entry, you will even win £100 and a set of mugs, as well as the honour of having your design placed on mugs and sold in Oxfam's 'Fair Trade' shops.

Oxfam is aiming at something different from a straightforward money-raising appeal. To find out what that is, it is necessary to read the text closely — which the intriguing picture encourages you to want to do. The answer eventually comes in the explanation of the idea of 'Fair Trade', with the message emphasised by the example of a banana farmer from the Caribbean, Felix Bernard. Oxfam is deliberately putting across a message that it is not simply trying to raise money. It is trying to help the trade and industry in less developed countries, so that they will be able to survive. By supporting the bananas which are produced by small farmers such as Mr Bernard, Oxfam is drawing attention to the difficulties which recent trends have created: 'Farmers can't compete with powerful transnational companies which have driven many of the world's smaller producers out of business.' It is a campaign aimed at changing our buying habits. We must, it seems, become sensitive to the economic hardships faced by many developing countries which supply us with our fresh fruit and vegetables. Oxfam is undertaking to place on the shelves of supermarkets products with the 'Fair Trade' label, so that we can support the cause not by donating money directly but by buying their goods. The competition is designed to start to make its audience more aware of the name 'Fair Trade' and what it stands for. It is appealing to our sense of justice and fair play: 'Buy them and you'll be Fair Trading.'

The 'Help the *Aged*' advertisement is a more direct appeal for money: 'Please don't turn the page'. The picture of a desperately hungry old woman from a Third World country, with the specific country not actually mentioned, is a well-used approach. 'Help the *Aged*' is not promoting some complicated social or economic policy. It is simply saying that £10 a month will keep someone such as Tsering alive. There is, however, an additional touch: the 'Adopt a Granny' approach. In recent years, charities have increasingly used this technique to make donors feel a greater sense of personal involvement in the charity. The same approach has frequently been used for children and animals.

The difference in approach is underlined visually. Oxfam's style is punchy, humorous, up-to-date. There are clear typefaces and an arresting picture, the man with a banana mouth, which arouses curiosity and makes complete sense only after reading the text on the reverse. 'Help the *Aged*', on the other hand, has a traditional appearance, a stark black and white photograph and a short, straightforward message. It is not necessary to do too much thinking: simply fill in a form and find out more.

The appeal of the Oxfam advertisement is very clearly aimed at school pupils, especially those aged from 14 to 18, and their parents or teachers. The 'Help the Aged' appeal is more general. No specific age-group is specified, although it might be thought that the reference to adopting a 'granny' would be aimed at those who were fairly young.

The principal difference between the two seems to relate to the amount of effort required to respond to the appeal. One plainly needs more reading, more thought, a subtle appreciation of the charity's tactics. It is necessary to go away and do something: create a design and think about a slogan. The other simply requires the filling in of a form. Not even a stamp is needed, since the address is FREEPOST. The difference between the two is really the contrast between a simple fund-raising appeal and an approach which aims to make the young reader think about world social and economic issues.

- **You have obtained two types of promotional literature on the subject of insurance (see pages 68–70). Compare the effectiveness of the two mailshots in making you want (a) to read them, and (b) to take the desired action.**

The APP accident insurance mailshot and the Barclays Insurance leaflet picked up in the bank are two examples of persuasive literature which are an increasingly common feature of modern life: the attempt to sell something, often either a product or a financial service. These two examples are also both concerned with insurance, and they are dealing with important aspects of life: sickness and health and car insurance.

There are also, however, important differences in the techniques of selling, the type of appeal, the layout and the design. The 'APP' medical insurance letter is said to be part of a larger pack which arrived through the door in a thick, packed envelope. The Barclays leaflet, directed primarily at Barclays customers, is designed to stand alone. 'APP' has several items, all of which are designed to reinforce the basic messages, with considerable repetition. The promoters of APP rely on people's curiosity to open an important envelope; Barclays hope customers will be attracted by the quality of the design of their leaflet.

The difference in visual layout of the information is striking. The APP pack starts with a letter, which is always 'personalised' to a named addressee – a common device made possible by new computer techniques. The actual appearance of the letter is of interest. It is clearly meant to look as though it has been produced on an ancient, battered typewriter. There is a great deal of 'typed' text on the page.

The Barclays leaflet is quite different. There is a large-type caption, which has a clear message: 'Whatever your renewal premium, we will beat it'. The subject-matter is insurance, and the emphasis is on quality and price. The text is clearly set-out, using modern design techniques; it looks professionally designed, with text and pictures strategically arranged.

In both cases, the object of the mailing is to attract someone to buy insurance, but in the case of 'APP' that message is decidedly more hidden. This may be because those selling medical insurance feel that they have to do more to get people interested. Barclays know that what they have to do is try to increase their own share of the car insurance market, by offering a deal which will tempt someone to transfer from their existing policy. Their sales pitch is therefore based on offering lower prices, quality, service and additional features. The advertisement stresses in particular what good value for money the Barclays deal is, and everyone wants value for money.

In the APP mailshot, the text trades on the fact that many people do not have medical insurance, and may not initially be interested. So the leaflet starts not by talking about insurance at all, but about the chance to win some money. It appeals therefore to the most basic 'something for nothing' instinct. The 'cash win' is mentioned in the very first sentence of the letter.

'APP' also plays on our fear that anyone can suddenly be struck by a disabling illness, and it tries to bring home to the reader just what a dreadful experience that can be without insurance. This mailshot is therefore not trying to persuade people to transfer from one form of medical insurance to another, but to take out private insurance for the first time, because of increasing concerns about health care.

Cash prizes are meant to 'hook' readers, so that they are more likely to stay with the scheme than leave it. Barclays, however, is using its 'name', as one of the largest international banks, to persuade customers who value its services to extend their loyalty. The effectiveness of 'APP' may well depend on how tempted the readers are by cash prizes. Some may feel that the chances of winning one of the large cash prizes are very slight. However, there will be others who are tempted. The Barclays scheme will attract those who want the cheapest car insurance, supplied by a successful bank. A 'guaranteed' low price is more tempting than the offer of a cash prize — probably a very small one!

Model answers: Question 2

- **Write a newspaper 'leader' or editorial based on the issues raised in the article (page 59).**

It's a dog's life... ... or death. And it could be a human's life. Or death.

That's why quarantine is a topic which arouses such fierce emotions. Since 1975, three thousand animals have died in quarantine, like Julie's English setter. And how many more are there like Anna's Jack Russell, put down by their owners rather than being allowed to go through the long and lonely months of quarantine?

But that is just one side of the argument. The other is that the risk to human life of <u>not</u> having quarantine is so serious that it is worth even such a heavy death toll of animals. After all, this country, unlike many others, has been free from rabies for a very long time.

This is why the story which we are carrying today matters so much. For the first time ever, thanks to the wonders of modern technology, we now have a real chance to end quarantine without opening the floodgates to a fresh invasion of devastating disease.

We say that the time is ripe for a change. Thanks to new vaccines and the latest silicon advances, a nightmare for pets and owners can be ended once and for all. The pets' passport scheme is a winner. It is safe and it is sensible.

The Government should introduce it, and do so as soon as possible.

We know from our readers all over the country that there is a long list of tragic tales and personal hardship. Many ordinary people, whose pets are just like members of the family to them, and who provide them with love and devotion, are daily affected by rules which we shall soon be able to tear up. These people will give a loud cheer to a government which has the courage to open up the cages and let out these long-suffering pets, provided they are in good health, so that they can be reunited at long last with their owners.

We say: these animals have suffered enough.

So have their owners.

Now is the time to end this example of man's inhumanity to man's best friend.

• **Write a letter to the managing director of the Leeds Castle foundation in which you set out your ideas for developing the site. You should analyse the possibilities offered by the buildings and grounds and comment on the advantages which your proposal will bring.**

1 Main Street
Hightown, Kent

The Managing Director
The Leeds Castle Foundation

Dear Sir

I have recently seen a copy of your leaflet, advertising 'The best day out in history'. It is an excellent leaflet, and the range of facilities is very impressive. I have spent a day with my family at Leeds Castle, and there is a great deal to do which is most interesting, such as the unusual 'Dog Collar Museum' and the complicated and baffling maze.

I believe that I can suggest something which will make even more of your superb site and facilities, and would like to put forward some suggestions.

It seems to me that you have the opportunity to make much more of the <u>educational</u> possibilities of Leeds Castle, while still preserving its appeal as an entertaining day out. Your leaflet stresses the castle's <u>history</u>, and you refer to the connections with 'Royalty and Romance', which Henry VIII represents particularly well. The displays about Henry and other royal figures are very well-designed.

It is this <u>historical</u> link which I think you can make more of. Henry VIII is the ideal figure to enable you to develop the site so that children from all over Kent and beyond will be drawn to Leeds Castle.

Now I know you might say 'The last thing we need is hordes of rowdy children tramping all over our castle and its beautiful grounds', but I hope you will listen to my ideas. School groups will be offered activities to stimulate them so that all pupils will be fascinated and fully occupied. The teachers themselves will love it, because the content of these sessions will really teach history in an unforgettable way. There will be trained instructors employed by the castle to help organise the visiting groups.

My proposal is called: 'Step into History, with Henry VIII and his six wives'. Pupils will go on an imaginative 'trail' through the site, exploring the variety of the castle's buildings and landscape. The latest museum technology, for example, will employ a wide range of computer-based activities, featuring historical objects for the children to feel and explore, and using high-class animations and models. There will be actors in costume, representing Henry and his wives. These actors know all about the history and life of their characters, so that they are able to act out scenes from history and answer even the hardest questions which the children will ask. Children will be able to ride across the lake in a boat which is a copy of a sixteenth century barge. In the gardens, near the grotto and maze, they will be able to watch Henry himself, trying to persuade the Pope to let him divorce Catherine of Aragon and marry Anne Boleyn, followed swiftly by a scene of Anne preparing for her execution on Tower Green.

These are just a few of my ideas. I am sure I can help Leeds Castle to live up to the proud boast of its slogan: 'The best day out in HISTORY'.

Yours sincerely

Robert Page

Model answers: Question 3

- **Write a letter to the leader of your local Council, Ms Brown. In this, you should try to persuade the council not to grant permission for the building of another out-of-town supermarket which you believe will ruin the shops in the High Street.**

Range of writing: **argue, persuade, instruct**

Rose Cottage
Oak Drive
Newtown
Middleshire

Dear Ms Brown,

This week, four more shops in our historic High Street have become empty. Soon, unless you take drastic steps, the High Street will become a wilderness, with nothing but banks, building societies and estate agents. Surely you must see the dangers! Can we not put a stop to the growth of out-of town monstrosities, which are draining away the life-blood of our town?

Action has to be taken now! For too many years, the Council has allowed the widespread destruction of the many small businesses which once made our town a varied and pleasant place to shop. Planning consents have been tossed out like confetti. The green-field sites on which superstores have been built have become a jungle of brick and concrete, while the derelict shops stand deserted, an eyesore to the dwindling numbers of loyal shoppers who struggle to keep our town centre alive.

The solution is obvious: no more supermarkets. The time has come to say 'No!'. It is high time that our Council made some hard decisions. Indeed, the moment is long overdue.

I ask you to think very seriously about this subject. Five years ago, within the space of 100 yards, my route along the High Street took me past a number of excellent retail outlets. I will now mention just a few.

A sewing shop used to exist which stocked everything from fine embroidery silks to odd buttons. Now I shall scour the streets in vain for these valuable items — and, of course, they are nowhere to be seen on the countless rows of supermarket shelves. In each store everything looks the same, whereas the old sewing shop had real character and variety.

A bakery provided high-quality early morning fresh rolls and croissants, as well as a wonderful selection of patisserie, not to mention old-fashioned English cakes and puddings. When will the younger generation have the opportunity to taste such delights?

I used to walk past a remarkable hardware shop, catering not only for the needs of the DIY enthusiast, but crammed with those indispensable items for helping with any domestic crisis. An enquiry for such things at the new DIY superstore is met, alas, only with a blank stare. Supermarkets do not give us that old-fashioned service that people still look for.

Now, of course, all of these interesting and valuable shops have gone. And these I have mentioned are only the tip of the iceberg. So change your minds before it is too late, especially for the hundreds of non-driving local residents who cannot reach the huge car-park-dominated supermarkets. Change your minds and policies before the town which you claim to serve becomes a hollow shell, rather than a living, bustling community.

Yours sincerely,

Elizabeth Granville (Mrs)

79

- **For a school Open Day, you have been asked to organise eight Year 11 (sixteen year-old) pupils to take a group of prospective parents on a tour of the school. Write a sheet of clear instructions which will enable them to perform this task well.**

INTRODUCTION

Remember that you have been specially selected for this important task, and that the school is relying on you. The job itself is basically a straightforward one. You are responsible for a group of ten parents. You must meet them, escort them and deliver them at the right place and at the right time, and you must keep to the precise course that you have planned, with no deviation. All parents MUST end up at the school canteen at 1600 hours (four o'clock) exactly, for tea with the Head of Year 7 and the Year 7 Form Tutors.

PLAN YOUR ROUTE

- Decide where you are going. The route should have <u>eight</u> points on it, chosen to show what the school has to offer.
- Draw out the planned route, showing each of the stopping-places and the expected time of arrival at each.
- Check your route carefully with all the other seven groups, to avoid the risk of congestion at any one point.
- Ensure that there is a five-minute interval, at least, between one group's departure and the next group's arrival at the most popular venues, such as the computer room. It is potentially disastrous if one group is trying to leave a room while another is trying to enter it.

KNOW YOUR SCHOOL

You need to be very well-informed about the school. Spend some time studying the relevant school documents, especially the Brochure which goes to all prospective parents, which your group will have with them. Be knowledgeable and be informative.

SPEAK TO PARENTS

It is absolutely essential that you give a good impression to the prospective parents, by your words and manner. We would like to encourage them to send their children to this school, not frighten them off! Answer their questions clearly, simply and with a smile. They may ask you about details of school policy which are beyond you. Invite them to raise these questions with the staff who will be available to deal with their queries over tea, or write in to the head-teacher.

ENJOY THE EXPERIENCE

Above all, I hope that you will find this a thoroughly enjoyable opportunity to show many different aspects of the school to our visitors, to talk sincerely and interestingly about your own experiences (but, please, not too many gory details!), and answer what will certainly be some fascinating questions. Have a really good time and remember: be prepared, be efficient and be friendly.

Glossary of media terms

Advertisements

Billboard – a board with posters or advertisements displayed

Brochures – small booklets with glossy advertising

Junk mail – post which is sent unasked by companies trying to promote or sell products

Leaflets – small, often folded sheets of paper carrying information or publicity material

Mailshots – the circulation of a leaflet, letter or advertisement

Poster – a large notice or advertisement displayed publicly, e.g. on billboards, often with a strong visual interest

Small ads – short advertisements in magazines or newspapers

Magazines

General – magazines for a wide readership, not on specialist topics

Specialist – magazines on a particular subject such as a sport or cars

Media Terms

Bias – showing favour to one side; directing or slanting material for a specific purpose

Caption – a headline or a few words or phrases accompanying text or a picture

Editorial/leader – a leading article in a newspaper or magazine, summing up on a main subject covered

Feature articles – articles in a newspaper or magazine which deal, often at some length, with a particular topic

Fonts – different type styles, e.g. italic

Graphics – use of visual effects, especially generated by computer

Headline – a bold heading to an article in a newspaper or magazine, summing up the subject

News articles – articles in a newspaper or magazine which tell the story of current news events, e.g. wars

Punning titles – titles with puns, which are often used in headlines or sub-headings to catch the reader's attention

Soundbites – short, snappy phrases or statements meant to be remembered easily

Sub-heading – a smaller heading than a headline, used in the body of an article to divide sections of the text

Types of Newspaper

Broadsheet – a large-page 'quality' newspaper, e.g. *The Times*

Local evening – a paper issued in the afternoon to serve a particular locality, e.g. *London Evening Standard*

National daily – an everyday newspaper, either tabloid or broadsheet, covering the country

Regional daily – an everyday newspaper, issued for a specific area, e.g. *Birmingham Post*

Sunday – a weekly paper, issued only on Sunday, e.g. *The Observer*

Tabloid – a small-sized newspaper, aiming for mass circulation, e.g. *Daily Mirror*

examination answers
together with examiners' comments

This final section of the book contains answers in both official examinations and in trials for the new material in *Tracks*. These are reproduced just as they appeared, including any spelling, punctuation or grammar errors. (These are generally underlined in the text.) The 'examiner's comments' show how the different answers fit the descriptions given for the various grades.

Paper 2F: Twentieth Century Poetry and Non-Fiction (Pre-Released Material)

The Foundation Tier Papers (2F and 3F) have a grade-range from C to G.

Question 1   *(20 marks for Reading)*

- **Look again at the poem *The Going of the Battery* by Thomas Hardy (in *Tracks*). Describe the scene of the soldiers leaving for war and explain how the wives feel. Give examples of how the language is used to:**
        build up the picture of the scene
        show the wives' feelings.

Main assessment objective: develop and sustain interpretations of text

Candidate's response

In the poem 'the going of the <u>battery</u>' by Thomas Hardy, he writes as though he is the wife of a soldier who must leave to go to war. He describes the whole scene of the soldiers and their wives travelling with them before they must leave them to go. He begins the scene with

'Rain came down drenchingly; but we — unblenchingly
Trudged on beside them through mirk and through mire'

By writing this the reader can already picture a scene of all these soldiers with their wives or girlfriends, trudging along through the rain on marsh land but not flinching or moaning because they know it must be done. Then you see how sad the situation is, because the wives are saying that both <u>them</u> and the soldiers are taking scarce steps as though they want to prolong their last moments together. Already Hardy has enabled the reader to get quite a clear picture of the scene in their minds, and the language he uses makes it easy to know what the wives are feeling.

[**Examiner's comment:** reference to language, but no detail or examples.]

Next Hardy describes the men all carrying their guns, looking up into the night. Everyone is silent as they reach the place where the soldiers and wives must depart from each other. The gas lighting glimmers drearily and lights up the wives' faces. The wives kiss their husbands and give them a last tight hug farewell. As they move away the wives sigh, blinded by their tears. As they all walk home again they pray for their husbands. They are all scared of <u>loosing</u> them and someone says;

'Nevermore will they come: evermore

Are they now lost to us'

This person is feeling <u>dispair</u>, she knows she may never see her husband again. But the wife in the poem has faith. She believes that god will guide them, that fate will make sure they will be okay. Yet, she says at night she hears voices, ghosts of the husbands, taunting her.<u>Trying</u> to make her believe the worst; but she knows she must believe they are well and wait, put trust in the <u>l</u>ord and see what happens.

Hardy builds up the scene by creating an atmosphere and using <u>discriptive</u> words which help the reader to get a vivid picture in their mind. He does the same to describe the wiv<u>es</u> feelings using words such as sad, weak, mad drearily, eerily, haunting, daunting and more to really make the reader understand the feelings of fear, sadness and hopelessness that the wives are going through.

In marking this question, examiners were looking for a focus on:
- ○ features of the scene, including physical description;
- ○ appreciation and interpretation of the women's emotions;
- ○ examples of Hardy's language to illustrate these emotions;
- ○ the evaluation of Hardy's use of language.

Examiner's comments

- **The language points are not fully developed** but there is a very clear understanding and comprehensive range of points.
- The answer **does not really evaluate language** in relation to the women's emotions.
- There are signs of personal response but **not much language analysis is offered**.
- There is reasonable awareness of the physical elements in the scene.

  GRADE AWARDED FOR THIS QUESTION: GRADE C

Question 2   *(20 marks for Reading)*

- **Look again at the extract from *Testament of Youth* by Vera Brittain (in *Tracks*). What strengths and personal qualities did Vera Brittain show in the way she coped with being a VAD (Voluntary Aid Detachment) nurse? Give examples from the text to support your views.**

Main assessment objective: read with insight and engagement

Candidate's response

Vera Brittain had everyone's life in her <u>hand's</u> and she didn't know <u>wheater</u> or not this job was <u>trueful</u>. All the people that kept coming and the people that they just hadn't got the room for. The <u>convey</u> came and they had to push people out of bed.

Vera really tried to keep <u>every-one</u> strengths up but they knew they were going to die. 'The only thing one can say is that such severe cases don't last long'. Her <u>personnality</u> towards the papers_she hated how the papers write there words.

Vera hated people that talk about god and the war. 'Yet people persist in saying that God made the war, when there are such inventions of the Devil about'.Vera had her days set out has she was the onlyVAD <u>T</u>here she was sisterVAD. It was a hard job but she kept her strength. 'Somebody said the other day that no-one less than god Almighty could give a correct definition of the jobVAD<u>.</u>. Most of her day was already taken with bed pans, and routine checks preparing the food and then the next lot came in. AllVera saw was horror and she couldn't do <u>nothing</u> about it when she first <u>start</u> she felt filthy<u>,</u> 'Never in my life have I been so absolutely filthy'. He was some-one which has to be about a hundred people e.g. VAD and orderly all in one. Vera when writing this it was a person that saw feelings_she gave all her thoughts to the letter she wrote to her mother.

In marking this question, examiners were looking for a focus on:
- ○ the capacity to evaluate the evidence provided about Vera Brittain's strength of character and qualities;
- ○ the ability to read text thoughtfully and use events and descriptions aptly to develop the response;
- ○ the use of evidence from the text to support the argument.

Examiner's comments
- A number of relevant points are made, but **these need fuller development**.
- There is some evidence of engagement and fair understanding, but the **writing is not totally clear in places**.
- The response quotes some evidence, but **could make greater use of this**.

GRADE AWARDED FOR THIS QUESTION: GRADE E

Question 3   (20 marks for Writing)

Range of writing: **inform**, **explain**, **describe**
- **Choose one of the experiences of war described in the prose passages you have studied in *Tracks*. Imagine you were caught up in this kind of situation. Write an eye-witness account of what you saw.**

Main assessment objective: use and adapt form for specific purpose

Candidate's response
It was early morning when I heard the message that the US rations had arrived I was over joyed myself and my kids had not eatern for 2 days. I went out minutes later to go and find some rations of food. I began talking to a refugee from around the corner she to was going for some food. It was then I found out that the package had landed on a mine field my first instinct was to turn back and go home but my children were so hungry I just had to go.

The refugees name was Zhina_she to had children she walked off in front. I was tempted to go back but couldn't bring myself to go back to the children with no food so I carried on. As I reached the field I saw people heading back with packages. I hoped I wasn't to late. I began to run but stopped when I heard an explosion A man had been picking up packages when he had stepped on a mine_he must have been dead as it looked pretty bad. I just wanted to go home at that point but carried on looking for any packages I could find_minutes later I heard another explosion_I was to scared to turn round so I carried on. It seemed that every couple of minutes a mine would go off_I couldn't take anymore. I had a couple of packages that would do I began to run suddenly I heard my name being called Lamona, Lamona

I turned round it was Zhina. She had her hands full of packages_I waited for her as she walked towards me when suddenly she stepped on a mine_it blew her legs of so I went to get help. Was anyone here to help me_No-one_I couldn't do anything to help her. I went futher on out of the field. The sights were terrible_many people were getting carried out on stretchers and some just lie there. Zhina was burried the following day.

I just wished the rations had fallen somewhere else.

In marking this question, examiners were looking for a focus on:
- ○ the ability to write in the required register;
- ○ convincing use of apt style to convey emotion, detail or setting;
- ○ good awareness of the need to communicate information and to describe and explain clearly the horrors of war and its effects in such areas as: housing conditions; food and drink; injuries and death; family life and relationships.

Examiner's comments

- There is quite a strong sense of an eye-witness account.
- The writing has a fair amount of detailed description and generally appropriate vocabulary, although **there is room for greater variety**.
- The organisation is reasonable.
- Control weaknesses are apparent, especially punctuation, and would keep it at no higher than a D; **there is a need for closer attention to accuracy in the writing and for careful checking**.

GRADE AWARDED FOR THIS QUESTION: GRADE D

Paper 3F: Media (unseen)

Question 1   (20 marks for Reading)

- **Study the advertisement which has been given to you.**
  In what ways does the advertisement try to persuade you that the Sinclair ZETA would be a good buy? Your answer should refer to:
    the type of information given
    the use of language
    the use of illustrations and graphic
    the overall design and layout of the advertisement

Main assessment objective: evaluate how information is presented (including use of presentation, structural and linguistic devices)

Candidate's response

The advert for the new Sinclair Zeta, try's to persuade you that the Sinclair Zeta would be a good buy it gives you a lot of information about the product. It tells you how to use the product 'To use ZETA simply touch the 'on/off' switch on the handle bar'.

It also gives you points on how long it lasts and how fast it can go aswell as giving you information about recharging the battery. The advert uses very good language which often makes you think about your past's with a bike,

"Have you ever cycled up a hill and had to get off and walk?"

This statement makes you look back at the past and makes you wonder if it would be easier if you had the new Sinclair ZETA

"Have you ever wished someone would come up with an igenious invention to take the effort out of pedalling when it gets to much."

Again this statement makes you think about togther the times when riding a bike has got to much, so it automatically makes you think if I had the new Sinclair Zeta than that wouldn't happen.

It also includes statements that make the Sinclair Zeta seem wonderful "it's a worlds first' 'like most brilliant inventions, Zeta is simplicity itself.'

'ZETA is so well engineered that it works well in all weathers.'

These <u>statement</u> persuade you that the new Sinclair Zeta is too good to be true making it seem like a <u>D</u>ream come true.

The use of illustration in this advert is very good_they are in colour so it makes the advert nice to look at. There is one major <u>D</u>rawing <u>P</u>laced <u>N</u>ear the top in the middle of the page_this <u>D</u>rawing shows how the Sinclair Zeta looks after it has been fitted in this <u>D</u>rawing_it also gives you information on the speed, <u>R</u>ange and the fact that you don't need any tax, insurance or a licence. This gives us a good idea of what it is going to look like.

There are also small illustrations over the page with points about the Sinclair Zeta. These are giving us details that are in the text. These are reminding us of some of the good points about the Sinclair Zeta which remind us and make us remember the Sinclair Zeta_also the illustrations are in colour so you tend to remember them more.

The general layout of this advertisement is very <u>G</u>ood_it tells you all about the Sinclair Zeta before informing you about the cost. Also the title of the advertisement is in <u>B</u>ig <u>B</u>old writing which attracts you to have a look.

'Take the slog out of cycling'.

This is the title of the advert after reading this really you are persuaded to look at the rest of the advert to see what it is about.

Overall this is a very persuasive advertisement which <u>uses the use</u> of illustration in a very good way.

In marking this question, examiners were looking for a focus on:

  ○ appropriate references to the text;
  ○ attempts to examine the details of the advertisement, to support judgements.

Examiner's comments

- This is detailed response, showing a generally sound grasp of intentions.
- The **erratic control of punctuation affects clarity**.
- Occasional insights push the standard towards C – **these are not consistent enough**, however.
- The response fits D Grade Descriptor: 'Shows generally sound awareness of some persuasive techniques', but in places **this could be more strongly developed**.

  GRADE AWARDED FOR THIS QUESTION: GRADE D

Question 2   *(20 marks for Writing)*

Range of writing: **analyse, review, comment**

- **A newspaper prints a story criticising the ZETA. Imagine you have used the ZETA. Write a letter to the newspaper giving your views. You should write about whether or not:**
     it is reliable
     it is easy to control
     its performance matches the claims in the advertisement
     it is good value for money
  You may also include any other relevant points.

Main assessment objective: use forms for specific purposes

Candidate's response

Dear Sir/Madam,

I am writing to you about the Sinclair ZETA. After reading the advert two months ago I decided that, being a person that uses bikes everywhere, the ZETA seemed like a brilliant buy. It would be an end to all of the problems they mentioned in the advert, but to my dismay it wasn't. As reliable as they said the ZETA was 'in all weathers', I'm afraid it just isn't. Although it has made some light relief of my efforts to pedal up a hill or ride into a stiff breeze, I've found that in wet weather the ZETA just doesn't work as well. Rain and muddy, wet tyres just don't work well with the ZETA.

Added to this is the controlling of the ZETA, it simply just isn't as easy as touching an on/off button, this is because sometimes the 'on' button just doesn't seem to work, either this or the ZETA just doesn't work up to its expectations. Another thing that bothers me about the ZETA is how long the battery lasts. Yes_it is easy to change, but once changed it hardly seems to last long. I feel that with full time use the 10 miles put in the advert is a bit of an exaggeration.

Although the ZETA isn't totally useless I feel that it is <u>no where</u> near the value for money I thought it would be when I ordered it. Unless all of the statements made about the ZETA in the advert were absolutely true, I don't feel that the ZETA is worth the £144.95 I <u>payed</u> for it. Considering the amount of work the ZETA does for me, which isn't much_I do not feel totally satisfied and will be asking for my money back. I think that your article which criticised the ZETA was a fair one.

Yours sincerely

In marking this question, examiners were looking for a focus on:
- how effectively the candidate had revealed an understanding of the requirements of the question;
- how effectively the candidate had used the written language to produce a relevant response;
- an appropriate tone and register in the writing.

Examiner's comments
- The range of points is very sound.
- The writing communicates clearly with good register and focus, with only occasional technical errors – sentence punctuation.

  GRADE AWARDED FOR THIS QUESTION: GRADE C

Question 3   *(20 marks for Writing)*

Range of writing: **argue**, **persuade**, **instruct**

- **Write an article for a magazine for young people using this title:** *Cycling: the best form of transport for the 21st century?*

Main assessment objective: adapt writing for a range of purposes and audiences

Candidate's response

The world is <u>poluted</u> cars, vans, <u>lorys</u>, buses, motor <u>biks</u>, and more are <u>poluting</u> the world just because people have to travel to work, <u>frends</u> home, school, <u>But</u> while you <u>traviling</u> in a transport which damages the earth the earth is getting weaker every minute because we choose to go in a car <u>wheel</u> why don't you use a more <u>enviromental</u> <u>aproach</u> like cycling. Cycling is enjoyed by billions_some people do it for fun_some people do it to save the <u>enviroment</u> but it is great fun <u>infact</u> more than 80% of the population have got bikes and they use then for <u>differn't</u> <u>thing</u>. Another great way to have fun is to go cycling with your family_not only it is fun_you get to exercise_<u>know</u> think_if you travel by car <u>your</u> damaging the <u>enverment</u> <u>your</u> not getting fitter but if you <u>rid</u> a bike as many people do you will not <u>damag</u> the <u>enviroment</u> you will get fit and it is much cheaper to get instead of a car_so why don't you tell your parents stop using the car and cycle. Remember it's your <u>choose</u> so pick the right one for you and for the world. <u>Infact</u> cycling is so popular <u>amoung</u> all ages and is more popular <u>the</u> 30 years ago so by the year 2000 we <u>predect</u> that more people choose to go and ride a bike not just for you for the earth_because if <u>to</u> much <u>polution</u> is in the world we will all die_so please help and let's make the world a happy ending.

In marking this question, examiners were looking for a focus on the quality of the candidate's writing, irrespective of the particular opinions which are expressed, including:
- ○ an attempt to argue a case and persuade the reader;
- ○ appropriate ideas, facts and arguments;
- ○ awareness of the interests of readers of a magazine for young people.

Examiner's comments
- There is **considerable technical weakness, including punctuation errors** (F criteria).
- The information and argument are reasonably clear and there is some capacity to fit the material to audience and purpose (E descriptors).
- **Accuracy and clarity of expression need closer checking.**
- **Sentences are not always divided correctly.**
  GRADE AWARDED FOR THIS QUESTION: GRADE E (JUST: E/F BORDER)

Paper 4H: Twentieth Century Poetry and Non-Fiction (pre-released material)

Question 1   (20 marks for Reading)

- **Look again at the poems *Dulce et Decorum Est* and *Anthem for Doomed Youth* by Wilfred Owen (in *Tracks*). How does Owen convey his attitudes to war in these poems? Support your answer with examples of Owen's use of language in the two poems.**

Main assessment objective: develop and sustain interpretations of text

Candidate's response
In 'Dulce et Decorum Est', Wilfred Owen explains that once you have experienced the sheer terror and horror of war, it is clearly not a lovely thing to die for one's country. In the first verse, he used language to give pictorial images of the exhausted soldiers, slowly <u>drudging</u> through sludge. When you read this poem, it does not occur to you that Owen has used enjambement, for every two lines the ending words rhyme, for example sacks, backs and sludge,

trudge. He uses soft sounding syllables such as drunk with fatigue. In this verse, they look like anything but soldiers, they have no need to move quickly.

The second verse is in contrast to the first as it starts with panic and desperation, it is full of action and sudden sheer terror as a man is too hesitant to cover his breathing from the gas. As a conclusion, Owen remarks on the fact that after you have witnessed such a tragic event, you cannot honestly believe that it is a good thing to die for one's country, that they realised that the man who died wasn't just a carcus, he taught them a serious lesson, this increases on the horror which has already been described.

'Anthem for Doomed Youth' has a religious aspect unlike 'Dulce et Decorum Est', as Owen often refers to bells, candles and prayers. When there was nothing else to save them, they could atleast rely on religion. This poem is a sonnet as it has a strict rhyming scheme, it is a celebration of despair. As the title describes, it is a patriotic song for the soldiers who went to war and had no chance.

In the first verse, he describes the loss of feeling and dignaty, no tenderness which is very harsh. He uses onomatopoeia which describes the sound of war. He uses negetive words to describe the pain some of these soldiers go through such as that there is no hope for them, they can pray contiuosly but nothing can save them from this. Prayers and bells are no comfort to them. At the end of this verse, the mood of the poem tends to soften and become slower. He sees no way out and asks himself; what can someone do to stop this?

The sentence, 'Shall shine the holy glimmers of goodbyes' is not tangeble, it is abstract and distorted. Then he goes on to recognise the sadness and paleness of war, the reflective and quiet mood at the end gives it rather a sombre conclusion as these people have inexpressable grief in silence, it hurts too badly to interpret how it feels. This poem I think is based on the shallow-ness of people's reaction to it, he has seen the worst and doesn't want to experience it again.

Owen makes us think more of the harsh situation that these soldiers are faced with and their reaction to the frustration of having no escape. At the end of his poems, he reflects the moods of people, what they have failed to realise or learnt and what kind of affect the scene has on him as if it was seen in a bizarre dream.

In marking this question, examiners were looking for a focus on:
   ○ candidate's appreciation and interpretation of the attitudes conveyed;
   ○ the selection of examples of language from the two poems to illustrate these;
   ○ the evaluation of language.

Examiner's comments
- There is a sustained interpretation with a reasonably clear structure.
- There is some comment on linguistic features, but this is not always fully accurate or clear.
- There are occasional technical errors, especially of punctuation, and awkward expression.
- The spelling is mostly sound, but flawed on more ambitious vocabulary.
- More examples and quotations would help to support the points made.
  GRADE AWARDED FOR THIS QUESTION: GRADE C

Question 2   *(20 marks for Reading)*

- Look again at the passages *Plymouth Hailed Victory At Midnight* and *The Schoolboy's Story* (in *Tracks*). In these two pieces, how important is close detail in building up pictures of first-hand experiences of war? Give examples of the vivid description of events.

Main assessment objective: read with insight and engagement

Candidate's response

The Western Daily Herald article pays great attention to detail throughout. This detail is used to draw the reader in, as it gives us a picture to visualise. For example:

'People poured into the streets. They danced, they sang, they cheered, they linked arms, strangers greeted and embraced one another.'

From all the adjectives that we are given in just two sentences we can create a clear picture, of what's happening, in our minds.

The adjectives in this article also make you read on as they are all positive. Such as jubilant and fun. The article has a 'feel good factor' which is created by the detail in which the article is written. As you read the article you start to feel better, as it is so well written, that you can feel all the emotions of the people in the article. The word celebration is used seven times in the passage which sums up the mood completely.

'The Schoolboy's Story' is written in first person. It is an eyewitness account of the war through a child's eye. As it is written through a child's mind a lot of things about the war are missed out, and all the detail is focussed on aeroplanes and scavaging for bits. Close detail is payed to all the planes, all the names are mentioned and there is a lot of focus on the machine guns. This passage really does give us a good insight into what the war was like for children.

The language is very simple, as you would expect from a child, yet due to it's content this passage is made readable for all ages. The close detail payed to his emotions is key to drawing us into the passage. For example, 'We got scared' and 'I would be in trouble'. This gives the passage an element of humanity and makes it believable.

In marking this question, examiners were looking for a focus on:
- ○ the capacity to evaluate the evidence provided;
- ○ the ability to draw on a thoughtful reading;
- ○ apt use of events and descriptions to develop the response.

Examiner's comments

- The response is well-focused, and has a good engagement with the events described.
- There is insight into attitudes.
- The candidate supports points (quoted) from the text, but **the argument and evidence could be developed more fully for the highest grades**.

GRADE AWARDED FOR THIS QUESTION: GRADE B

Question 3 *(20 marks for Writing)*

Range of writing: inform, explain, describe

- **Imagine you are a television or radio reporter covering an event in a war you have read about in Tracks or an event in any other war. Write the report which you intend to broadcast, using an appropriate style and tone. Explain the situation and describe important incidents which you have seen or heard about from eye-witnesses.**

Main assessment objective: use and adapt form for specific purpose

Candidate's response

Here at the BBC we have just been informed of an incident which could change the world forever.

Nuclear weapons have been an ever increasing threat recently as more and more countries have <u>aquired</u> them to protect themselves. Despite this increase I do not feel that any of us really expected them to be used.

Today has seen the coming of the nuclear age as America dropped the first nuclear bomb on Hiroshima, Japan, earlier today.

The total devastation is not at this moment known but it is believed millions are dead with the number increasing as the radiation spreads.

The blast could be seen from miles away and one eye-witness described it:

"A massive cloud of dust swelled up from the site and increased in size as it engulfed Hiroshima and the surrounding areas."

Another eye witness described the site:

"There was nothing there but barren wasteland. No life to be seen in the once thriving town of Hiroshima. People, animals, trees, houses — everything has been destroyed.

The whole world stands in shock as we see, first hand, the destruction that nuclear weapons can have. We must use this to learn from and hope that other countries will have the sense never to use such destructive weapons again."

Let us all hope that this will, at last, bring an end to the last six years of conflict throughout the world and that peace will survive for our life time and many life times to come.

As further information is found we, at the BBC, will bring it to you as soon as we can.

In marking this question, examiners were looking for:
- ○ the ability to write in the required register for broadcasting;
- ○ convincing use of apt style;
- ○ good awareness of the need to communicate information and to describe and explain clearly.

Examiner's comments
- The response is fluent and immediate.
- Good use is made of eye-witness accounts.
- There is a useful sense of an overview from the 'BBC correspondent'.
- The use of language is concise, evocative and effective.
  GRADE AWARDED FOR THIS QUESTION: GRADE A

NB The quality of this answer fully meets the Grade A criteria; if there had been a slightly fuller exploration, it might well have met those for the A*, since the engagement with the task and material is excellent. An appropriate tone and register are captured convincingly.

Paper 5F: Media (unseen)

(20 marks for Reading)

- Study the two leaflets which have been given to you. One was produced by the Whale and Dolphin Conservation Society (WFDCS) and the other by the Royal Society for the Protection of Birds (RSPB). Each leaflet tries to persuade readers to give money to the charity. Compare the persuasive techniques used in the leaflets. You may wish to comment on the following but are free to refer to any other relevant points:

  the ways in which the subject matter is organised and presented

  the use of language

  the design and layout of the leaflets

  reasons why you consider one leaflet to be more accessible than the other.

Main assessment objective: evaluate how information is presented (including use of presentational, structural and linguistic devices)

Candidate's response

Both the WDCS brochure and the RSPB brochure attempt to attract and persuade the reader into sending money to save the dolphins and birds respectively. Each uses many methods of persuasion, from physical rewards in return to money sent, to emphasising the beauty of the animal.

Both have very appealing covers: the WDCS brochure uses a well-taken photograph of two dolphins rising out of the water simultaneously, attempting to illustrate the 'beauty', 'intelligence' and 'friendliness' of the dolphins, words used to complement the photograph in the brochure itself; the RSPB also uses a very well-taken photograph of a large group of physically beautiful birds, looking grand in mid-flight, to illustrate to the reader the beauty of that which will be supported by the funds. This is a very common, yet persuasive method, used in many brochures and advertisements.

One <u>noteable</u> difference, again on the cover, is that the WDCS brochure uses words as well as pictures to persuade the reader to continue reading the brochure, while the RSPB <u>belives</u> that a more persuasive method is to use less writing, but larger and to the point, simply stating the cause of the charity and the name of the Society, "Help save our BIRDS and wildlife... join the RSPB now." Then in an attempt to attract the attention of people that revel in the chance to receive free goods, states in the top right-hand corner of the brochure, "Free <u>birtable</u>".

Once both brochures are opened it becomes evident that two very different styles are used. In the RSPB brochure, the information given is categorised under five different headings: The first, "The work of the RSPB", is an attempt, not only to state the work of the society but also to make the reader feel guilty, and make him believe that it is his fault that many of these beautiful birds are dying and losing out; the second 'The benefits to you', is again aimed at the audience that needs to benefit <u>himself</u> in order to help others. This is the same audience that the 'free birdtable' was aimed at. This is just a list of benefits, from 'Free access' to nature reserves to "knowledge that you are helping conservation"; this is then followed by the application forms and on the back three pages of the brochure: the RSPB states the membership prices, immediately followed by <u>reasurence</u> that one would receive that 'FREE' birdtable in return; and a list of ways that 'Your support enables us to:'. On the other hand the WDCS uses the brochure to explain the running of the society; to give information on eight different dolphins available for adoption; to tell the reader how unique and exciting this process is; and finally, at the back, the application form.

One method of <u>benefitting</u> the presentation and atmosphere is the use of browns, greens and other colours we <u>asociate</u> with forests, trees and nature.

The WDCS uses a more attractive language, with words such as "thrill", "beautiful", "fascinating" and "wonders". While the RSPB uses language such as "Free", "your benefits", "we need your support", emphasising that this process benefits both us and 'you'.

Altogether I found the WDCS more attractive because I preferred the presentation of it, and the methods they used, in my eyes, were more persuasive to the reader and I was particularly <u>taken in</u> by the use of information on each dolphin.

In marking this question, examiners were looking for:
- ○ a focus on how particular techniques were used to persuade the readers;
- ○ insight into the language and other textual features.

Examiner's comments

- The candidate shows a good understanding of the two leaflets and requirement of the question, but for **an A grade the evaluation could have been a little more convincing**.
- Effective points are made.
- There are **some technical slips which suggested room for more careful checking** – high B.

GRADE AWARDED FOR THIS QUESTION: GRADE B

Question 2 (20 marks for Writing)

Range of writing: **analyse**, **review**, **comment**

- **Imagine you are employed to raise money for either the WDCS or the RSPB. Write about three advertising methods which you would use. Explain what you see as the advantages and disadvantages of each of your chosen methods. You may wish to consider any of the following:**
  National newspaper advertising, local newspaper advertising, direct mail shots, posters, press releases, leaflets, billboards, or some other form of advertising.

Main assessment objective: use and adapt form for specific purpose

Candidate's response

As an employee of the RSPB, a society which relies heavily on public support, using persuasive advertising would be a very important part of my job. My aim would be to convince as many people as possible, without exhausting the resources of the Society. I would primarily use three methods of advertising; magazine advertising, television advertising, and advertising in national newspapers. Millions of people regularly watch television and read magazines and newspapers.

To use television advertising effectively would require very careful planning. The advertisements would be long enough to be persuasive, yet not too long, resulting in too much expense. The advertisements would have to explain how the RSPB helps to protect birds from disease, pollution and other problems, yet graphic images might not be allowed until after the watershed. Instead I would choose to concentrate more on the good work of the Society than on the plight of birds without public support from the RSPB. Beautiful images of birds flying over stunning scenery would stir up emotions in many people. The advertisements would also have to show the benefits of joining the society. Viewers could see families enjoying days out at RSPB reserves, or reading the free magazines. Any other free offers would be shown, such as the free bird table described in the leaflet. I would have to choose also the times at which the advertisements would be most effective.

The main advantage of this advertising would be that the public would see, without the effort of reading, the advantages of membership of the RSPB. The advertisements would also be seen by a huge number of people. After all, people often don't read advertisements in leaflets yet they rarely switch off the television when they find one advertisement boring. As a free phone number would be given to the viewer as a way to join, he would not be confronted by any time_consuming filling in of forms. The main disadvantage would be the huge expense of producing and then showing the advertisements, which could cost the RSPB a huge sum of money.

The use of national newspaper advertising would be a lot less expensive. The advertisement would also be seen, though not necessarily read, by a huge audience. The advertisement would probably have to be in black and white, so I would concentrate primarily on text rather than photographs or other images. It would be important to use a large text size and to give the reader, as concisely as possible, reasons why he would join the society. It would be good to describe any special offers to encourage the reader to join or to send off for more information. An order form or freephone telephone number would be included. It would also be important to include the logo, which is well known and respected, in a prominent position. This would show the reader that the advertisement is for a well trusted, long established charity.

The newspaper advertising would be less expensive and would reach many people who do not watch television regularly. It would also be easier to produce the advertisement. The main disadvantage would be that a lot of people would inevitably not read or would completely ignore the advertisement. The advertising would therefore have less effect than television advertising.

Advertising in certain popular magazines would be another relatively inexpensive form of advertising. Advertisements could be in full colour and take up a whole page or a double page spread. The magazines would be selected so that readers would be known to like birds, animals or wildlife in general. For example an advertisement in 'National Geographic' would be far more useful than the same advertisement for the RSPB in 'Vogue'.

The magazine could be a good format for large glossy photographs of birds in their natural habitat. Equally, it would be possible to show the suffering of birds in graphic detail. The format would also allow a good amount of large text, so many arguments could be used. The advertisements could also include order forms which the reader could easily cut out. Any offers and the membership pack could be shown with photographs and bright text to be very persuasive. This form of advertising would therefore reach the smallest audience of the three, but would also be likely to convince the highest percentage of that audience to join.

In marking this question, examiners were looking for:
- a clear analysis of three different methods used by fund-raisers;
- evaluative comment on advantages and disadvantages of each;
- clear and precise use of language.

Examiner's comments
- The candidate analyses advantages and disadvantages in a sharply-focused and arresting manner.

- Analysis is 'assured and well-constructed'.
- Overall, the answer meets the descriptors for Grade A*: a pleasure to read for its lucidity and control.

GRADE AWARDED FOR THIS QUESTION: GRADE A*

NB This response captures a fully convincing register, combined with close analysis and comment, evaluating advantages and disadvantages effectively. It has also been checked carefully to ensure accuracy in spelling and punctuation.

Question 3   *(20 marks for Writing)*

Range of writing: **argue**, **persuade**, **instruct**

- **Write a speech for a classroom debate on a topic about which you feel strongly. You could choose a local, national or worldwide issue.**

Main assessment objective: adapt writing for particular purposes and audiences

Candidate's response

Today I am going to talk about the way that the media <u>continally</u> makes people feel that they have to live up to certain visual images_they do this by constantly giving us images of people with perfect bodies. Teenage magazines don't totally exclude people who don't fit in to this image as they do <u>oftern</u> have <u>feature</u> on larger model_but <u>altough</u> they do this it is <u>oftern</u> seen as a <u>once off</u> feature rather than a constant presence in the magazine. By making a big deal about big models they are saying that it's not the norm.

This isn't just a feature of teenage magazines_most <u>womens</u> <u>magazine</u> constantly have a diet feature making you feel guilty unless on a diet or exercising.

This is part of the reason which makes people feel that they must diet or feel depressed and eat more. There are other examples of the way that the media mistreat people this is a problem that not only <u>affect</u> <u>girl</u> there has been recent <u>publisity</u> for the fact that 1 in 4 <u>bulimac</u> and <u>anerexic</u> are boys.

I am not saying that all models should be big because again this is giving a single visual image which is the main problem_the lack of differences_and this <u>doen't</u> stand for just size_many teenage magazines in particular don't give enough positive images for African and Asian girls_for disabled people and even girls that where glasses_these magazines should include a fair cross section. Some magazines have claimed that this is because aren't enough of these models but if they were to ask for them then the model <u>agenises</u> would be forced to sign the girls.

<u>Unfortunatly</u> I feel the only way we can really change the way that these magazines reflect society is by boycotting them. As all media <u>is</u> <u>primaly</u> based around making money the only way to <u>effect</u> them is where it hurts in the pocket.

And it may seem that one person can't have any <u>affect</u> if every person who felt the same was to do something constructive then it would make a difference.

In marking this question, examiners were looking for:

- answers which showed an understanding of the purpose of the speech and an awareness of audience;
- responses which set out the issues clearly and identified the speaker's particular perspective.

Examiner's comments

- This definitely has some suitable argument and persuasion.
- There are **a number of errors in expression and accuracy of spelling and punctuation**, despite 'some awareness of audience and purpose' – Grade D descriptor; for the higher grades, **the writing would have needed greater clarity and control, and a more varied and subtle vocabulary**.
  GRADE AWARDED FOR THIS QUESTION: GRADE D

Acknowledgements

We are grateful to the following for permission to reproduce copyright material:

Anvil Press Poetry for 'War Photographer' by Carol Ann Duffy from *Standing Female Nude* (1985).

Barclays Insurance Services Co Ltd for extract from car insurance brochure, 1998.

Victor Gollancz Ltd, and Mark Bostridge and Rebecca Clare Williams, the literary executors of Vera Brittain for Vera Brittain: extract from *Testament of Youth*, (first published 1933), copyright © Literary Executors of Vera Brittain 1970.

The Guardian for article by Maggie O'Kane, 'Desperate Bosnians' from *The Guardian*, 27.11.93, Copyright © The Guardian 1993.

Help the Aged for 'Adopt a granny' advertisement.

David Higham Associates for 'The Second World War' by Elizabeth Jennings from *The Poetry of War 1914-1918* (BBC & Longman).

Leeds Castle Enterprises Ltd for day visitor leaflet, 1998.

Newsgroup Newspapers for article by Neil Syson: 'Cyber pets will escape quarantine' from *The Sun*, Monday 21.9.98. Copyright © The Sun 1998.

Oxfam Publishing for Oxfam's Fast and competition leaflet, Oxfam GB 1998.

Random House UK Ltd for 'The Send-Off', 'Dulce et Decorum Est', 'Anthem for Doomed Youth', 'Disabled', and 'Inspection' by Wilfred Owen, all from *The Complete Poems and Fragments* (Chatto and Windus, 1983) edited by John Stallworthy.

Alan Ross for 'Night Patrol' from *Blindfold Games* (Collins Harvill 1986).

PHOTOGRAPHS:

Carol Ann Duffy: by Chris McKee, courtesy of Anvil Press.

Thomas Hardy: courtesy of Dorset County Museum, Dorchester.

Elizabeth Jennings: courtesy of Carcanet Press.

Wilfred Owen: courtesy of The English Faculty Library, Oxford and the Owen Estate.

Aldridge Press; Gordon Dickerson (Tony Harrison); Geoffrey Wadsley; Virago (Maya Angelou).

Copyright permission for the following has been sought, but at the time of going to press copyright holders had not responded. The publishers will be happy to make the necessary arrangements on request at the earliest opportunity.

Katherine Tynan: 'Joining the Colours' from *Scars Upon My Heart* (Virago Press).

Dennis Winter for the extract from *Death's Men: Soldiers of the Great War* (Penguin, 1978), Copyright © Dennis Winter 1978. The extract includes quotations from S Millard and Adele Comandini: *I Saw Them Die* (Harrap, 1936), and from H Allan: *Toward the Flame* (Harper, 1934).